Virtual Reality, Artificial Intelligence and Specialized Logistics in Healthcare

Authored By

Yui-yip Lau

Division of Business and Hospitality Management
College of Professional and Continuing Education
The Hong Kong Polytechnic University
Hong Kong

Tang Yuk Ming

Department of Industrial and Systems Engineering
The Hong Kong Polytechnic University
Hong Kong

&

Leung Wai Keung Alan

Hong Kong Funeral Logistics Ltd
Hong Kong

Virtual Reality, Artificial Intelligence and Specialized Logistics in Healthcare

Authors: Yui-yip Lau, Tang Yuk Ming and Leung Wai Keung Alan

ISBN (Online): 978-981-5179-99-6

ISBN (Print): 978-981-5196-00-9

ISBN (Paperback): 978-981-5196-01-6

need for a court order if at any point you breach any terms of this License Agreement. In no event will any delay or failure by Bentham Science Publishers in enforcing your compliance with this License Agreement constitute a waiver of any of its rights.

3. You acknowledge that you have read this License Agreement, and agree to be bound by its terms and conditions. To the extent that any other terms and conditions presented on any website of Bentham Science Publishers conflict with, or are inconsistent with, the terms and conditions set out in this License Agreement, you acknowledge that the terms and conditions set out in this License Agreement shall prevail.

Bentham Science Publishers Pte. Ltd.
80 Robinson Road #02-00
Singapore 068898
Singapore
Email: subscriptions@benthamscience.net

BENTHAM SCIENCE

CONTENTS

FOREWORD

This book focuses on the innovations brought to the healthcare sector by virtual reality, artificial intelligence, and specialized logistics. The book chapters discuss how emerging technologies can advance healthcare research, improve the management of patient records, facilitate human remains logistics, development of innovative applications for vulnerable population groups, and improve health monitoring of different patient groups. Furthermore, several book chapters discuss how new-generation technologies can be used to overcome some of the major challenges caused by the COVID-19 pandemic (*e.g.*, the design of resilient supply chains in the wake of frequent pandemics, anti-pandemic measures to prevent the virus spread across the communities, how to provide a safer environment in the senior citizen homes under the pandemic conditions, micro-business simulation models for healthcare products). We expect that this book will provide a fresh outlook on the latest technologies in the healthcare sector and how they can be effectively used in different settings. Findings, examples, and recommendations presented in the chapters will be helpful to the community and a wide range of stakeholders in the healthcare sector.

Maxim A. Dulebenets
Department of Civil & Environmental Engineering
Florida A&M University-Florida
State University (FAMU-FSU)
College of Engineering
Tallahassee, FL 32310
USA

PREFACE

The design of this book aims to enrich policymakers, researchers, students, and industrial practitioners' knowledge and skills of advanced technologies (*e.g.*, virtual reality, artificial intelligence, and macro business simulation) and specialized logistics (*e.g.*, human remains logistics and vaccine logistics) in the healthcare industry. As such, we illustrated various real-life examples to demonstrate across different chapters. In general, this book is divided into nine main book chapters. Chapters 1 and 2 mainly address the state-of-the-art in healthcare research. As such, artificial intelligence, computer information systems, the Internet of Things, and 3D printing are further investigated in the healthcare research in Chapter 1. Digital health with smart Internet of Things technologies is further explored in Chapter 2. The specialized logistics are provided in Chapters 3 and 4. The human remains logistics are comprehensively discussed in Chapter 3 while the vaccine supply chain is thoroughly explained in Chapter 4. Both the aforementioned chapters have been covered in the context of COVID-19. Since the COVID-19 pandemic has created a new page in human history, we illustrate real cases and memorable photos to show how the local community implements various anti-epidemic measures in Chapter 5. Chapters 6, 7, and 8 are relevant to the trending issues of the elderly. Chapter 6 mainly focuses on homes for the aged during the COVID-19 pandemic. Chapter 7 mainly concentrates on the use of advanced mobile apps for the elderly in the 21st century. Chapter 8 mainly provides a narrative review of mobile technology from the older adults' perspectives. Chapter 9 addressed the adoption of macro business simulation on healthcare products *via* the use of hand sanitizers as illustrative examples.

The first author expressed the happiness of forming a new interdisciplinary research team across logistics, health, and engineering disciplines. This groundbreaking research provides a foundation work on future research work. Also, the first author would like to appreciate the unreserved support from his wife, colleagues, students, and friends.

The second author indicated that this book is successful and can enrich the teaching pedagogy and illustrate the real cases in learning materials. The updated knowledge definitely increases the academic and managerial implications.

The third author would like to express special thanks to my lovely wife Poon. She stayed at home with me all the time while I wrote in the evenings, even on Sundays and holidays. My lovely wife sacrificed too much for me.

Yui-yip Lau
Division of Business and Hospitality Management
College of Professional and Continuing Education
The Hong Kong Polytechnic University
Hong Kong

Tang Yuk Ming
Department of Industrial and Systems Engineering
The Hong Kong Polytechnic University
Hong Kong

&

Leung Wai Keung Alan
Hong Kong Funeral Logistics Ltd
Hong Kong

CHAPTER 1

The Revolution of Immersive Technologies in Healthcare Research

Abstract: In the digital era, many technologies such as artificial intelligence (AI), computer information systems, Internet of Things (IoT), Industry 4.0, immersive technologies, 3D printing, *etc.* are being adopted to facilitate operations, provide better management, and enhance workflow and working efficiency. As such, digital health technology and management are the key topics that are attracting wide attention, since it is important both in enhancing efficiency and safety. In fact, most of the healthcare and medical care tasks cannot be replaced entirely by computers. The training of healthcare workers and medical practitioners still remains important. Immersive technologies including virtual Reality (VR), augmented reality (AR), and mixed reality (MR) are widely adopted in numerous industrial and training applications. VR provides a fully immersive experience for the trainees, while AR and MR provide interactive stimulation while maintaining attention in the physical world. Despite the types of immersive technologies used for training, healthcare training, and medical simulation are key components of digital health technology. Nevertheless, in many cases, a trainee's acceptance and behavioural training in participating in immersive training are still uncertain. Understanding their acceptance and behaviour is important not only in developing effective simulated training but also in enhancing their autonomy and motivation in participation. To this end, we also introduce some of the research models that are commonly used to support health and medical training and simulation.

Keywords: Augmented reality, Healthcare, Immersive technology, Mixed reality, Research model, Virtual reality.

1. INTRODUCTION

Healthcare and medical care are the most important and essential services for any developing society worldwide. They are not only critical for promoting, maintaining, and managing the health of society, as well as preventing disease, but the item also plays a major role in reducing unnecessary disability and death. In recent years, due to the rapid increases in the size of the elderly population and the aging problem globally, the shortage of healthcare workers continues to be serious in many countries. A direct way to tackle such issues is to increase the number of healthcare workers. However, recruiting and training in healthcare

Yui-yip Lau, Tang Yuk Ming & Leung Wai Keung Alan

are always difficult issues due to the lack of healthcare trainers. Cultivating and training healthcare workers are very important in order to ensure the quality of healthcare services and to ensure the safety of patients so that they can recover as quickly as possible.

In the digital era, much of the workload can be replaced and reduced with the latest technologies such as artificial intelligence (AI) [1], computer information systems [2], Internet of Things (IoT), Industry 4.0 [3], immersive technologies, 3D printing [4], *etc.* Notwithstanding that the technologies can facilitate healthcare operations, improve management, and enhance workflow and efficiency, most of these tasks cannot be replaced entirely by computers, particularly in the training of healthcare workers. Immersive technologies including virtual Reality (VR) [5, 6], augmented reality (AR), and mixed reality (MR) [7] are widely adopted in numerous industrial applications [8]. They have been recently widely adopted in medical and healthcare aspects due to the features of the simulated scenarios and situations that may not be created in traditional real-life training. For instance, VR can be used to mimic sudden changes in virtual environments, external stimulations, display digital cadavers, *etc.*

In this book chapter, we illustrate the latest developments in how immersive technologies can be applied in practical healthcare applications in aspects of medical and health training. On the other hand, regardless of the virtual technologies that have been proven to be effective in many types of research, the practices in healthcare research are not widely documented. Indeed, research that investigates the effectiveness of medical and healthcare training is essential in the design of training programme, as well as in determining the immersive content that can provide better training effectiveness. Here, we first provide an example of how immersive and simulation technologies can be potentially applied in healthcare training. Then, some research background is given to provide insight to readers on how healthcare research can be conducted accordingly. This provides useful insight to the readers that can be further extended to healthcare, medical care, or other related applications.

This chapter is organized as follows. A brief introduction to the importance and the latest technologies in medicine and health is given in section 1. Then, the current applications of immersive technologies in virtual training are given in section 2. Section 3 elaborates on the keys to conducting healthcare research and the theoretical model that is commonly used in technology-based user acceptance research.

2. APPLICATIONS FOR IMMERSIVE TECHNOLOGIES

In the last two decades, VR has been increasingly used for entertainment, education, healthcare, manufacturing, design, aviation simulation, *etc*. VR has proven successful in healthcare and medical simulation due to the difficulty and cost of creating physical and real models for conventional training. VR offers a lot of advantages in terms of cost efficiency and outcome effectiveness in many aspects. Particularly, VR enables the creation of digital content and mimics random simulation to provide more effective and immersive training to participants. Thus, VR training in health and medical care is mainly derived from virtual training and simulation-based training which are elaborated in the following.

2.1. Virtual Training

Foronda *et al.* [9] noted that advanced virtual simulation technologies can be utilized in surgical nurse training. For instance, CliniSpace gives a three-dimensional computer simulation of a healthcare setting. The "world" is a clinical environment, such as an intensive care unit, an office, a clinic, or a patient's home. It is a web-based, multiuser system, so several students can log in from any location using their own laptops. Students choose a character, or "avatar," such as a nurse. The use of a headset with a microphone allows them to be heard by others in the clinical setting and engage in real-time conversation while working with a patient and accompanying equipment. Verbal interaction between distantly logged-in people creates a sensation of immersion and physical presence. Digital Clinical Experience (DCE), developed by Shadow Health as a consequence of academic research conducted by nursing, medical, and allied health schools, is another example. The DCE is a collection of Web-based, asynchronous virtual patient simulations for the development and evaluation of clinical reasoning abilities in nursing. Autonomous, three-dimensional, virtual patients with realistic speech and motion inhabit the DCE's virtual environments, each being able to identify and reply to more than one hundred thousand inquiries. This technology enables students to generate their own patient interview questions, find opportunities for empathy and patient education, and arrange their virtual patient's physical examination. The DCE is extremely useful for teaching physical assessment, communication, clinical reasoning, and nursing processes. Another is vSim, which is primarily intended for nursing instruction. vSim for nursing was created in partnership with Laerdal, Wolters Kluwer Health, and the National League for Nursing. This Internet-based, single-user software allows students to practice cognitive nursing skills in a virtual environment. Learners will be capable of assessing a patient, reviewing instructions, administering drugs, and performing nursing interventions. When the patient responds to therapies, students are able to evaluate and learn from their mistakes. This virtual simulation enables individuals to learn in their own time and in the comfort of their own homes, as well as to rectify and repeat the simulation until mastery is achieved.

In the fields of medicine and nursing, the virtual operating room is regarded as an effective instrument for training technical and non-technical issues. Bracq *et al.* [10] conducted a study using a simulation scenario to test error recognition in a virtual operating room, intending to improve situational awareness, determine whether the VR operating room can improve the nontechnical aspects of the nurses, and assess overall perceptions of the virtual operating room. Eighteen scrub-nursing students and eight experienced scrub nurses were placed in a simulated operating room and instructed to report any deficiencies they encountered. It was determined that those who recognized more errors had a higher level of situation awareness, identified high-risk errors more quickly, and were more engrossed in the virtual operating room than those who discovered fewer problems. The outcomes also revealed a decrease in burden and an increase in nurse satisfaction, as they investigated the operating area more than specialists did and discovered more errors, particularly those that were somewhat hazardous, and virtual simulation proved acceptable and inspiring to students. Georgieva *et al.* [11] investigated the practical implementation of a 360° virtual environment for a clinical laboratory, a central laboratory for sterilizing, and a virtual operating room to study the benefits of VR in nursing education. It was determined that the primary benefits of the 360-degree shooting technology are that it allows students to learn about the hospital environment in general and allows for the speedier completion of practical exercises that require multiple repetitions and instructor explanations. In addition, the use of virtual reality in medical training has a great deal of potential for nurses who are learning a variety of procedures and manipulations that must be performed correctly, safely, and promptly. Students can use VR technologies to perform these operations in a simulation that creates scenes from the real world (Fig. **1**).

In today's hospitals, a patient is treated by a team of specialists employing complicated collaborative processes and techniques, rather than by a single practitioner, which is a cause of concern. This indicates that a student must practice not only patient-and-nurse communication but also complex exchanges between experts, such as while preparing a patient for surgery. To address these issues, a comprehensive and adaptable alternative that facilitates practice and exploratory learning experiences is required. However, Kleven *et al.* [12] provided an exploratory study regarding the use of a virtual university hospital comprising both medical and non-medical participants as a place for learning, doing research, and fostering innovation. The room was designed to resemble of one of the most contemporary university hospitals, St. Olav's University Hospital in Trondheim, Norway. The study also investigated the use of the Oculus Rift, a head-mounted display that facilitates immersion in the virtual operating room. The majority of poll respondents who tested the Oculus Rift felt it to be a more engaging and fun method of learning, with a higher sense of presence and immersion. In addition, the researchers concluded that a virtual university hospital (VUH) should ideally serve as a hub for both medical and non-medical education and that a VUH should initially support educational activities for medical professionals and students, such as procedure training, visualizing treatments, and examinations, and anatomy lectures.

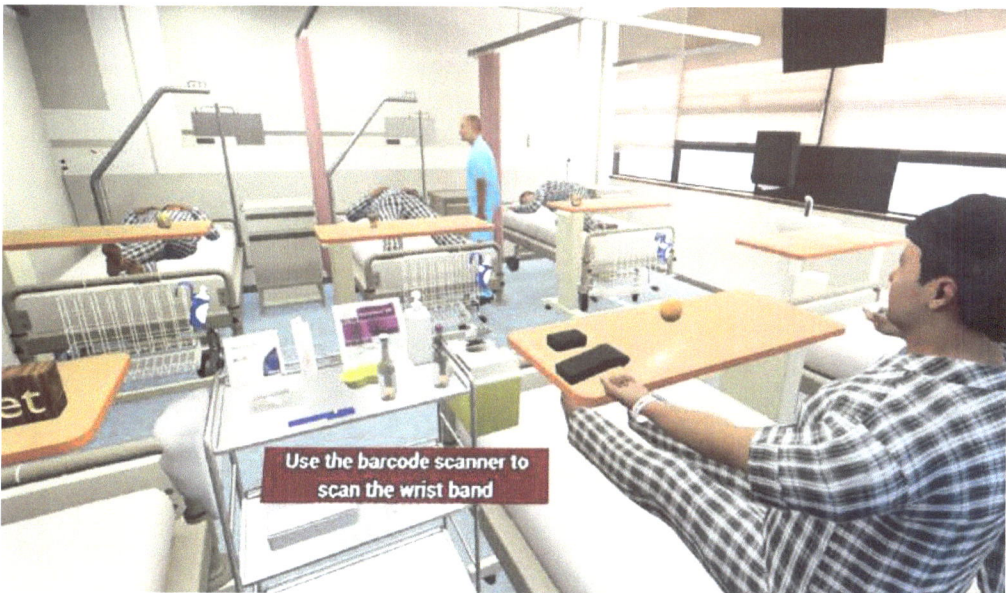

Fig. (1). vSim for nursing.

2.2. Simulation-based Training

Simulation refers to an artificial model of a real-world process utilized to achieve certain learning outcomes through experiential learning. Simulation-based medical education refers to any educational activity that utilizes simulation aids to simulate clinical circumstances [13] (Fig. **2**). Wittmann-Price *et al.* [14] created a project that recognizes and promotes veteran nurses to seek a bachelor's degree in nursing by acknowledging their unique skills, knowledge, and attitudes. Nine concepts or competencies were verified for course credit by nursing professors. The principles were then evaluated by simulating their application. Simulation in a hybrid format (using manikins and standardized patients) was chosen as the evaluation mechanism in a controlled context because of its capacity to operationalize the constructivist theory of learning in an experiential learning scenario. Karataş and Tüzer [15] studied the impact of simulation-based training on the confidence and contentment of nursing students caring for isolated patients. After completing a pretest, the student's initial performance was evaluated using a low-fidelity simulator. Following this, there was theoretical teaching. In an appropriate circumstance, each student in the study group interacted with a standardized patient who was under contact isolation. Then, debriefing sessions with groups of five students were held. After completing the application, the students were given a post-test to evaluate their satisfaction and self-esteem. It was determined that this permitted the provision of training and care while protecting patient safety and honoring their rights. In contrast to clinical practice, where such a technique would be unethical, the strategy enables students to learn from their mistakes by permitting them to experience the natural consequences. Following the training, the scores of the nurses' critical thinking, self-confidence, and skills all increased dramatically. In addition, simulation training has been demonstrated to increase self-confidence and self-esteem. In terms of the nurses' perspective, Awad *et al.* [16] attempted to elucidate the perceived usefulness of simulation technology in nursing education. It was determined that the majority of students have positive attitudes toward using simulation technology in nursing education and training. Interestingly, female students had more positive attitudes about simulation technology than male students, which could be because female students are more likely to be interested in technology. Simulators also enhance one's sense of self-worth.

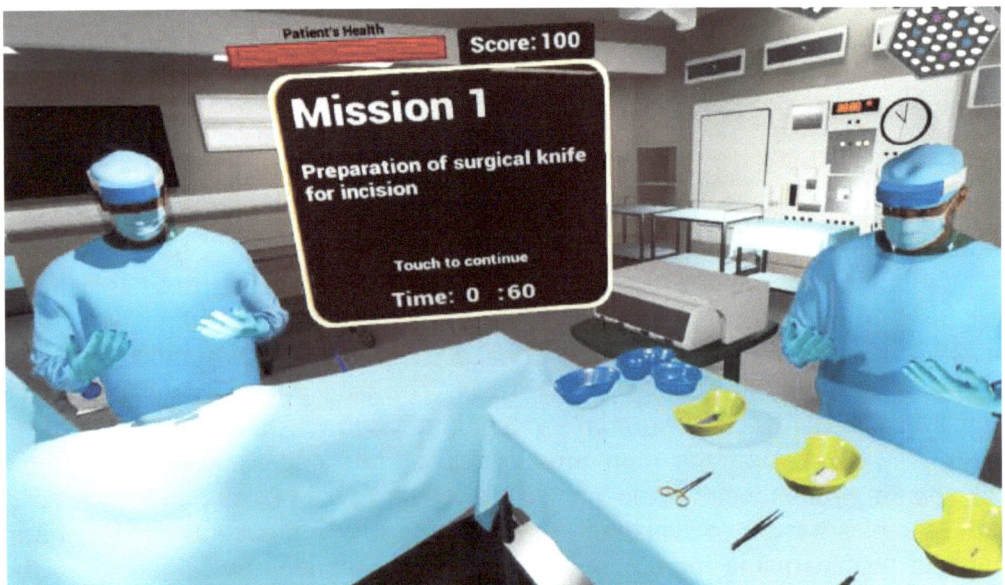

Fig. (2). Simulation-based training.

2.3. Surgical Simulation

Virtual reality (VR) could serve as a suitable substitute for cadaveric temporal bone surgical dissection courses, which are an integral part of otolaryngology residents' training. Mickiewicz *et al.* [17] examined the virtual reality temporal bone surgery simulator during a simulation of antro mastoidectomy. The VR system was based on the Geomagic Touch Haptic Device from 3D Systems. The study was designed as a prospective trial with three VR simulation training sessions in which 11 otorhinolaryngology trainees and four ENT physicians with no prior surgery expertise performed virtual dissections on a VR temporal bone model. The effectiveness of the VR system was demonstrated by an increase in performance quality and a decrease in errors, as well as the indication that VR training should be incorporated into medical training programs because it provides a structured, safe, and motivating environment to learn complex anatomy and practical skills. Endotracheal Intubation, a life-saving treatment that requires putting a tube into the trachea (windpipe) through the mouth to preserve an open airway and permit artificial respiration, has also profited from technological advancements. It is a difficult psychomotor skill that requires substantial training and knowledge to avoid difficulties. As a just-in-time training platform, Rajeswaran *et al.* [18] designed AirwayVR, a virtual reality (VR)-based simulation trainer for beginners to study and practice endotracheal intubation and for professionals to mentally prepare for a hard case before surgery. AirwayVR was developed in UnityTM and runs on the virtual reality device HTC ViveTM with two-hand controls. The hand controllers are used to interact with the virtual reality learning environment and make use of the many available resources.

To maximize and expedite the productivity of new employees in the medical device manufacturing industry, skill training is essential. Ho *et al.* [19] introduced and evaluated a self-adaptive and autonomous virtual reality training system for the assembly of hybrid medical devices. This system incorporates AI, virtual reality, and gaming principles, and enables training to occur in a virtual work cell without the need for a physical trainer. As a sort of hybrid medical device, a Carbon nanotubes-polydimethylsiloxane (CNT-PDMS) based artificial trachea prosthesis is used as a case study to demonstrate the usefulness of the system. The findings of the evaluation demonstrated that the suggested system may effectively impart skills and information to users, boost the participants' sense of accomplishment, shorten the time required to learn new things and train and eliminate any costs associated with hiring a physical trainer.

2.4. Health Professions Education

In the realm of health professions, education, and skill training are essential for maximizing the productivity and professionalism of healthcare staff. However, as a result of these needs, various underlying issues occur, including contamination and safety problems, a lengthy training period, high skill and experience requirements for operators, and greater training costs [19]. Consequently, immersive learning, such as virtual reality, augmented reality, and 360-degree video, is widely recognized as a useful tool for the development of physical skills in the training of health professionals (Fig. **3**). Patel *et al.* [20] conducted a study to determine which training approach, *i.e.,* lecture, a virtual world operating theatre, or a simulated operating suite (SOS), would be more beneficial for novices in training for their first visit to the operating room for the introductory session based on knowledge from a theatre induction curriculum developed to guide the education. The study revealed considerable improvements in the virtual world operating room and simulated operating suite groups. With just a few hours of instruction, beginners' knowledge, abilities, and attitudes toward the operating room can all be enhanced. If such a curriculum were implemented as a supplement to the World Health Organization's undergraduate curriculum on patient safety, it might potentially improve the quality of care from the outset. Immersive and realistic training environments, such as the SOS, provide novices with the most useful experience conceivable. Abelson *et al.* [21] proposed a novel virtual reality team training system to determine if it was possible to create a virtual reality operating room to simulate a surgical emergency scenario and to test the simulator for construct facial validity by modifying ICE STORM, a virtual reality system capable of simulating a variety of health-care professionals and settings. Using ICE STORM to simulate a common surgical crisis scenario, participants were required to remedy four factors responsible for the loss of laparoscopic visibility. The results demonstrated that the participants found the training environment to be realistic and the simulation to be stimulating. All participants felt that the simulation's workload was manageable. It was determined that the building of a virtual reality operating room for surgical team training is feasible and can provide a realistic setting for team training.

In addition to surgical emergencies, VR applications also include paramedic emergencies. In their research, Schild *et al.* [22] exhibited a multi-user virtual reality (VR) system that aims to give novel paramedic training tools that supplement conventional learning methods. The hardware configuration consists of a two-user, full-scale VR environment with head-mounted displays for two interactive trainees and an additional desktop computer for a trainer participant. The software generates a networked multi-user environment that presents a paramedic emergency simulation with a focus on anaphylactic shock, a representative scenario for urgent medical cases that occur too seldom during a standard vocational training term. The prototype enables several individuals to participate in paramedic training as trainees or instructors in a co-located or remote virtual environment and demonstrates how Virtual Reality may be utilized to increase hardware quality in vocational training.

Fig. (3). Virtual reality medical training.

The COVID-19 outbreak wreaked havoc on in-hospital medical education, leading to the prohibition of medical students in their first year from accessing hospitals. Virtual reality that simulates the clinical setting can alleviate this challenge, and it can be especially useful to enhance traditional hospital-based medical education during the pandemic. De Ponti *et al.* [23] evaluated how a cohort of medical students felt about fully virtual learning, which included simulations of clinical settings during the pandemic. It was determined that the change in the teaching modality prevented the interruption of medical training, and the majority of students who participated in the study felt that this teaching approach was of excellent quality. In addition, the majority of students who attended the session reported that the teaching style was effective and met their expectations. In addition to typical training at the patient's bedside, the findings indicated introducing online access to these materials for future maintenance. Frost *et al.* [24] conducted a second study to investigate the mixed reality (MR) learning experience of Bachelor of Nursing sophomores. The research focused on a specific sort of MR that projects a holographic picture into a real classroom using a head-mounted display (HMD). The assessment results confirmed the efficacy of this developing technology, demonstrating that MR can aid in the development of clinical judgment in student nurses. Additionally, when used in pairs, it has the potential to enhance students' ability to build professional discussion while describing a patient's state to another health professional, as well as their ability to recognize physical signs. Students are able to view patient symptoms and have unlimited exposure to events without patient risk or suffering, which is a significant advantage of this sort of virtual learning experience.

Based on the existing literature, it is apparent that the use of digital technologies, such as virtual reality (VR) and simulation, for health professions training is becoming increasingly popular, with some studies evaluating the attitudes of students or health professionals toward advanced training methods. Even though the application of digital health technologies has been extensively investigated in recent years, the vast majority of studies have not addressed the evaluation of participant's perceptions by observing their autonomous behavior while completing the VR training program. In addition, there have been numerous inadequate healthcare studies on research models to measure the efficiency of digital technology-based training. Consequently, there is an incentive to conduct additional healthcare research.

3. HEALTHCARE RESEARCH AND MODELS

In healthcare research, there are two key approaches: qualitative and quantitative methods. The quantitative approach is the process of collecting and analyzing numerical data and is usually used to discover patterns and generalize results from various population groups. The qualitative approach usually involves collecting and analyzing non-numerical data such as text, video, or audio to understand concepts, opinions, or experiences. The questionnaire, interview, and focus groups are some of the approaches for conducting qualitative research. Recently, the mixed approach integrating qualitative and quantitative methods has also been adopted in many studies. The questionnaire is a good medium for data collection using the mixed approach. In spite of the methods used for healthcare research, virtual reality and simulated training in digital health usually involve understanding user acceptance and behaviour before and after conducting the tests. In this regard, a research model is very important to study user behaviour in the examination scientifically. There are several commonly used research models for investigating user acceptance and behaviour in digital health and technology adoption. The research models and the selection considerations are elaborated in the following sections.

3.1. Technology Acceptance Model (TAM)

One of the most important theories of technology adoption is the Technology Acceptance Model (TAM) [25], which states that two key elements influence a person's intention to use new technology: perceived ease of use and perceived usefulness (Fig. **4**). The subjective probability that using a given application system would improve one's work performance within an organizational environment is described as perceived usefulness (U). The degree to which the prospective user expects the specific system to be effort-free is referred to as perceived ease of use (EOU) [25]. For example, an older person who thinks that digital games are too hard to play or a waste of time will be less likely to adopt this technology, whereas an older adult who believes that digital games provide the required mental stimulation and are simple to learn will be more willing to learn how to use them [26]. TAM claims that attitude, which is a combination of perceived usefulness and perceived ease of use, is the most important factor in a user's behavioral intention and actual usage. Many studies of user acceptance have scientifically validated the causal links between these constructs [27].

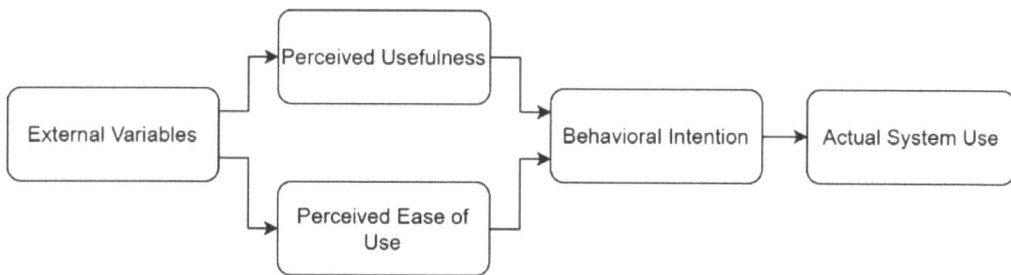

Fig. (4). Technology acceptance model.

Accelerated use of TAM has been seen to examine learners' intention toward using virtual reality (VR) as an autonomous learning tool. Autonomous learning or self-regulated learning is "an active, constructive process whereby learners set goals for their learning and then attempt to monitor, regulate, and control their cognition, motivation, and behavior, guided and constrained by their goals and the contextual features in the environment." [28]. Huang and Liaw [29] proposed a research model, based on the TAM model, perceived self-efficacy, perceived interaction, and learning motivation to test learners' motivation and intention on using an E-commerce virtual reality learning system (ECVELS) within a constructivist paradigm. Students can access various individual learning subjects in a 3D virtual stimulated scenario according to their preference based on six learning topics: logistics, cash flow, online marketing, e-commerce types, information security, and mobile commerce. The result illustrated that the theoretical conceptual model integrating constructivism and TAM is effective for realizing learners' perceptions of the usefulness of virtual reality learning environment. Perceived self-efficacy and perceived interaction are both key elements influencing perceived ease of use, usefulness, and learning motivation in such environments. Furthermore, perceived ease of use, perceived usefulness, and learning motivation are all important elements in determining whether or not learners will employ virtual reality learning environments. A structural equation model based on TAM was built by Hsu *et al.* [30] to examine the relationships among the variables about the use of the wearable virtual reality language-learning platform for English learning and to determine the impact of these variables on students' behavioral intentions. It was concluded that self-efficacy had a direct impact on students' views of the wearable virtual reality technology's ease of use, as well as an indirect impact on perceived usefulness, attitude, and behavioral intention. It also suggested that since self-efficacy was such an important factor in student technology use, educators should work to improve student self-efficacy in order to encourage them to explore new technology. Al-Azawei *et al.* [31] introduced a VR game-based e-assessment application to evaluate learners' understanding of self-learning courses. To conduct the study, they compared and contrasted the experiences of students using two different e-assessment technologies: a VR game-based e-assessment system and a Moodle quiz tool by using two constructs of TAM: perceived ease of use and perceived usefulness, alongside learners' performance and perceived playfulness. The students were separated into two groups, one of which utilized the Moodle tool and the other used the suggested VR application. It was expected that the integration of game-based learning (GBL), which means providing students with games that have instructional objectives that can be met through gaming, can motivate learners and enhance their experience in learning in the evaluation process. It was found that even though there were no differences statistically in learners' performance, perceived playfulness, and technical ease of use, there were substantial differences between the two groups. Another research study that evaluated learners' acceptance of VR learning was conducted by Huang *et al.* [32], who proposed a web-based 3D VR interactive learning system developed for undergraduate medical students to learn about human physiology, particularly the parts of the body. It was designed to be utilized with desktop VR and projection-based VR in order to accommodate self-learning, with the goals of aiding students in comprehending the structure and function of a virtual body and allowing students to examine 3D organ items from various perspectives and uncover spatial correlations between them. To investigate learner attitudes towards learning through VR technology, the study validated the relationship between three traits of VR (Interaction, immersion, imagination) and the key elements of TAM. It was concluded that the immersion and imagination characteristics of VR-mediated course content have a favorable influence on perceived usefulness and can anticipate perceived ease of use, both of which contribute to learners' behavioral intention to utilize VR learning systems.

Apart from virtual reality, the use of the virtual world and augmented reality is also measured by the Technology Acceptance Model to investigate the factors that influence the learners to use them. A study conducted by Ali *et al.* [33] used the constructs from TAM and extended factors such as computer playfulness, computer self-efficiency, and computer anxiety to examine students from the University of Bahrain of their intention to use Second Life (SL) - a costless, downloadable online 3D virtual world created by Linden Labs in which users use their avatars to navigate, interact and learn within the environment. The results of the investigation suggest that most of the students accepted the application of SL as it was useful and easy to use. In addition, the results show that perceived ease of use influences users' willingness to embrace SL *via* perceived usefulness. Computer self-efficacy, computer playfulness, and computer anxiety are all important predictors of the perceived ease of use of the virtual world. Another research study by Iqbal and Sidhu [34] focused on solving the problem of inadequate learning efficiency and long-term learning retention for acquiring dance skills by using augmented reality technology based on constructivism learning theory and the Technology Acceptance Model (TAM). The proposed system ARDTS was developed for all levels of dance learners, from novice to intermediate to advanced for self-learning. TAM, as the evaluation model together with other factors such as enjoyment, was utilized as a tool to examine the acceptance and influencing aspects of ARDTS in promoting a certain dance technique among a group of people from varied backgrounds and interests.

3.2. The Unified Theory of Acceptance and Use of Technology (UTAUT)

Other than TAM, the Unified Theory of Acceptance and Use of Technology (UTAUT) is a popular contemporary adoption theory that is useful for testing technology acceptance and adoption. The four potential constructs that describe user perception and acceptance behavior, according to the UTAUT model, are performance expectancy, effort expectancy, social influence, and facilitating conditions, with four moderating factors: age, gender, experience, and voluntariness of use [35] (Fig. **5**).

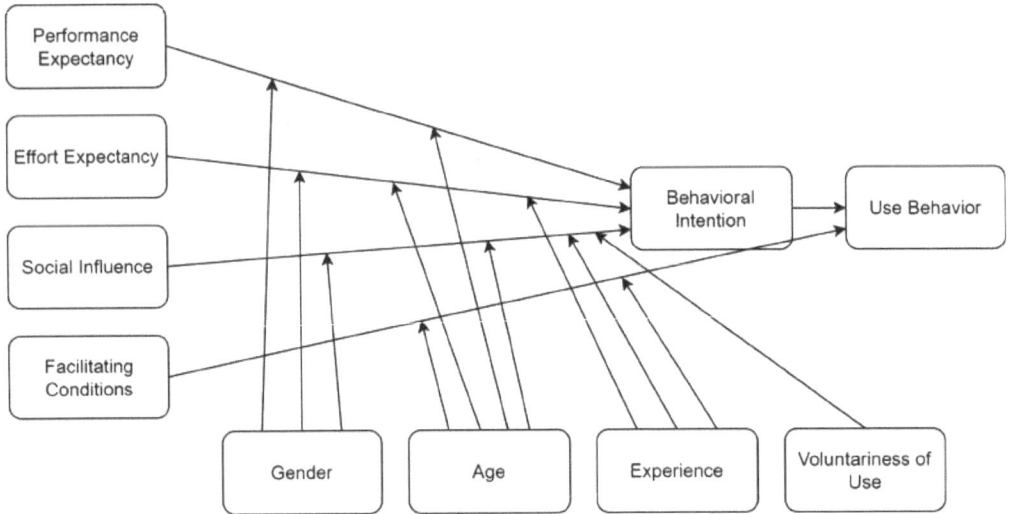

Fig. (5). The unified theory of acceptance and use of technology (UTAUT).

A study was performed by Bracq *et al.* [36] using the Unified Theory of Acceptance and Use of Technology (UTAUT) paradigm to examine the acceptability and usefulness of a novel VR simulator for procedural skill training by scrub nurses, as well as examine which factors were linked to the behavioural intention to use the VR simulator and see if there were any variations between expert and non-expert users. To test the simulator training system, a scenario was created to teach 13 expert scrub nurses from the neurosurgery department of a French University Hospital and 16 non-expert users how to set up the instrumentation table in the operating room for a craniotomy. After the simulation session, the system's non-instrumental aspects, as well as participants' reactions, were evaluated by assessing their subjective workload, sense of presence, the level of simulator sickness, and asking them open-ended questions. The results showed that the VR simulator's acceptability was established with no discernible difference between experienced scrub nurses and non-experts. Age, gender, or skill had no bearing. All participants evaluated workload, immersion, and simulator sickness identically and praised it for its teaching value, enjoyment, and realism. Shen *et al.* [37] explored the direct determinants that influenced students' motivations for using wearable head-mounted displays (HMDs) in learning by using the four factors of the unified theory of acceptance and use of technology and the four modes of Kolb's learning styles. According to the findings, all four UTAUT components had a positive and substantial influence on students' behavioral intention to employ HMDs in learning, however only the concrete experience mode of Kolb's learning styles had a positive and significant effect.

3.3. Theory of Planned Behaviour

The Theory of Planned Behaviour (TPB) is a psychological theory that is derived from the Theory of Reasoned Action (TRA) [38, 39]. Individuals make rational, reasoned judgments to engage in certain behaviors by analyzing the information available to them, according to both theories. The behavioral performance is decided by the individual's intention to engage in it, which is influenced by the importance of the individual sets on the behavior (attitude), the ease with which it may be executed under his or her control (perceived behavioral control) and the perspectives of relevant individuals (subjective norms) [40] (Fig. **6**).

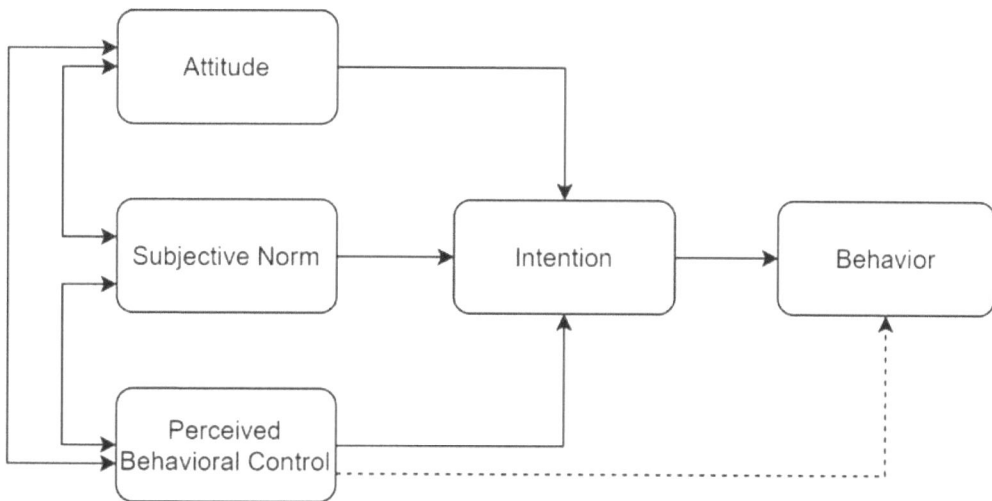

Fig. (6). Theory of planned behaviour.

The use of TPB has successfully anticipated and explained a wide variety of human behaviors and intentions, including autonomous behaviors in using advanced technologies as a method to learn. Virtual reality (VR) is being studied and used in education in a variety of sectors to extend educational options and improve learning. Fussell and Truong [41] conducted research to find out what factors impact students' intention to use virtual reality in a dynamic learning setting, as well as their acceptance of VR by constructing an expanded TAM and including variables from Ajzen's theory of planned behavior (TPB) that are significant for evaluating VR technology. The researchers suggested that the strongest connections were seen in the initial TAM factors and the model was a helpful tool for figuring out how students feel about utilizing virtual reality in a dynamic learning environment. In addition, researchers might modify this model for use in other dynamic educational or training situations where virtual reality is being evaluated as an educational tool. Kwok *et al.* [42] introduced virtual reality-based crisis management training for staff to practice digital twin-based crisis management, which can offer a great amount of vital information about the crisis to emergency personnel and is a necessity in complex manufacturing systems. To investigate the fundamental factors that influence how users perceive and use virtual reality for crisis management training, a research model adopting the Technology Acceptance Model (TAM) and Theory of Planned behavior (TPB) was proposed in the study. The findings revealed that users' attitude towards the VR-based training system and their perceived behavioral control were both directly significant to their behavioral intentions, implying that a positive attitude towards using the system and a sense of having enough control over the system were good starting points for stimulating the intention to try the system, which supported the Theory of Planned Behavior.

At the beginning of the teaching revolution, e-learning marked the latest stage in remote education. With the increasing popularity, research investigating the underlying mechanism of students' intention and acceptance has climbed to a new level. Zhou [43] integrated the theory of planned behavior (TPB) and the self-determination theory (SDT) as a research model to examine the cognitive and psychological factors that affect Chinese university students' choice to use Massive Open Online Courses (MOOCs) for learning. It is concluded that attitudes toward MOOCs and perceived behavioral control (PBC) were important drivers of MOOC usage intention. The controlled motivation was an antecedent for only subjective norms, but the autonomous motivation was an antecedent for all three TPB core components. Mouloudj *et al.* [44] conducted a study to analyze students from Algerian Universities on their motivation to acquire knowledge online during the COVID-19 pandemic by utilizing the theory of planned behavior (TPB). After collecting data from 214 college students in 6 universities in northern Algeria, it was found that students' intentions to adopt online learning systems are positively influenced by attitudes, subjective norms, and perceived behavioral control (PBC). The findings aligned with the TPB framework, which highlighted the importance of TPB constructs in predicting and explaining intentions in the context of the COVID-19 pandemic and online learning, which could benefit the development of an effective online learning system for educational institutions in the face of health crises. Another study done by Lee [45] synthesized the expectation–confirmation model (ECM), the technology acceptance model (TAM), the theory of planned behavior (TPB), and flow theory to develop a theoretical model to explain and forecast users' intentions to continue employing e-learning in the future. The study demonstrated that satisfaction had the greatest impact on users' desire to continue, and on perceived usefulness, attitude, concentration, subjective norm, and perceived behavior control, all of which were significant yet weak predictors.

Mobile technology advancements are quickly broadening the scope of learning in areas outside of formal education (*i.e.,* informal learning) by enabling flexible and instant access to rich digital material. Within formal education, mobile learning (m-learning) may also play a vital complementary role. Cheon *et al.* [46] studied the present situation of college students in the United States about their perceptions toward mobile learning in higher education by using a conceptual model based on the theory of planned behavior (TPB) to explore how their beliefs impact their intention to use mobile devices in their coursework. In the study, they assigned external beliefs to three types of constructs in the context of m-learning: attitudinal, normative, and control, which are the antecedents of the attitudinal constructs that affect the intention to employ m-learning. The findings revealed that the TPB adequately described college students' adoption of m-learning and provided important implications for improving college students' adoption of mobile learning. More specifically, their intention to embrace mobile learning was positively affected by their attitude, subjective norm, and behavioral control. Tagoe and Abakah [47] used the theory of Planned behavior and TAM's perceived ease of use and perceived usefulness to underpin the investigation of students from the University of Ghana Distance Education students' of their m-learning readiness as they prepare for the roll-out of the school's m-learning curriculum for distance students. After analyzing questionnaires from 400 students, the results confirmed the notion of planned behavior control's relevance in assessing students' m-learning readiness, and it was necessary to pay greater attention to control beliefs such as perceived self-efficacy and learning autonomy. Moreover, the high levels of attitudinal beliefs (perceived usefulness and perceived ease of use) indicated that students who believed m-learning was simple to use would employ it.

3.4. Research Model Selection

To use a theoretical framework that contains TAM or TPB, certain criteria must be taken into account, and there is a need to be aware of the multiple limitations that exist. One of TAM's limitations is the variable that refers to a person's behavior, which must be examined over subjective indicators such as behavioural intention and interpersonal impact. However, social influence is the subjective norm referred to when a person is affected by "word of mouth" from a coworker or a friend but without handling social issues or social demands. The second drawback of TAM is that, due to diverse subjective factors such as societal values and standards, individual traits, and personality attributes, underline behavior that is impossible to measure accurately in an observed study. As a result, a family's or friend's argument that can affect technology use may be influenced by demanding social influence that is highly manufactured. Even if the notion is true in principle or for the individual use of innovation, it may not be trustworthy or exact in a working context [48]. For TPB, LaMorte [49] pointed out that the limitations include: 1) Regardless of the intention, it is assumed that the individual has gained the opportunity and resources necessary to be effective in undertaking the desired behavior. 2) Other factors that influence behavioral intention and motivation, such as fear, anger, mood, or prior experience, are not taken into account. 3) While it considers normative influences, it ignores environmental and economic variables that may impact a person's intention to perform an action. 4) It considers behavior to be the result of a linear decision-making process and ignores the possibility of changes over time. 5) While the addition of the construct of perceived behavioral control made a significant contribution to the theory, it says nothing about actual control over behavior. Despite the limitations mentioned, researchers have used certain TPB elements and added other behavioral theory components to make an integrated and more comprehensive model. According to Mathieson [27], both models could be very effective when being integrated by assuming a system is created to serve users in a variety of functional domains. TAM might be used by an analyst to locate dissatisfied users and learn about their issues in general because of its general constructs (usefulness and ease of use), which are likely to be relevant to most individuals, regardless of their functional area. On the other hand, TPB can give additional precise information that is specific to the group when a group of particularly disgruntled users is discovered. To put it another way, the general information TAM gives might help indicate areas where it would be beneficial to have more specific information from TPB.

CONCLUSION

This book chapter introduces some applications of immersive technologies for virtual and simulated training. The virtual training also includes the practices of health workers and medical practitioners, as well as patients. The simulated training includes surgical simulation to provide practice for surgeons. Health professionals' education using immersive technologies is also elaborated, and some of the research approaches in digital healthcare are explained. Various technology acceptance research models and users' behavioral models are also elaborated to provide insights to readers on how digital health training research can be conducted to enhance the training effectiveness and motivation in participating training [2].

REFERENCES

[1]   Li W, Tang YM, Yu KM, To S. SLC-GAN: An automated myocardial infarction detection model based on generative adversarial networks and convolutional neural networks with single-lead electrocardiogram synthesis. Inf Sci 2022; 589: 738-50.
[http://dx.doi.org/10.1016/j.ins.2021.12.083]

[2]   Li W, Tang YM, Wang Z, Yu KM, To S. Atrous residual interconnected encoder to attention decoder

framework for vertebrae segmentation *via* 3D volumetric CT images. Eng Appl Artif Intell 2022; 114: 105102.
[http://dx.doi.org/10.1016/j.engappai.2022.105102]

[3]   Tang YM, Chau KY, Fatima A, Waqas M. Industry 4.0 technology and circular economy practices: Business management strategies for environmental sustainability. Environ Sci Pollut Res Int 2022; 29(33): 49752-69.
[http://dx.doi.org/10.1007/s11356-022-19081-6] [PMID: 35218493]

[4]   Mo JPT, Tang YM. Project-based learning of systems engineering V model with the support of 3D printing. Australas J Eng Educ 2017; 22(1): 3-13.
[http://dx.doi.org/10.1080/22054952.2017.1338229]

[5]   Fong K N K, Tang Y M, Sie K, Yu A K H, Lo C C W, Ma Y W T. Task-specific virtual reality training on hemiparetic upper extremity in patients with stroke. Virtual Reality 2021; 26(2): 453-64.

[6]   Tang YM, Ng GWY, Chia NH, So EHK, Wu CH, Ip WH. Application of virtual reality (VR) technology for medical practitioners in type and screen (T&S) training. J Comput Assist Learn 2021; 37(2): 359-69.
[http://dx.doi.org/10.1111/jcal.12494]

[7]   Tang YM, Ho HL. 3D modeling and computer graphics in virtual reality.Mixed Reality and Three-Dimensional Computer Graphics. IntechOpen 2020.
[http://dx.doi.org/10.5772/intechopen.91443]

[8]   Fong KNK, Tang YM, Sie K, Yu AKH, Lo CCW, Ma YWT. Task-specific virtual reality training on hemiparetic upper extremity in patients with stroke. Virtual Real 2022; 26(2): 453-64.
[http://dx.doi.org/10.1007/s10055-021-00583-6]

[9]   Foronda CL, Alfes CM, Dev P, *et al.* Virtually nursing. Nurse Educ 2017; 42(1): 14-7.
[http://dx.doi.org/10.1097/NNE.0000000000000295] [PMID: 27454054]

[10]   Bracq MS, Michinov E, Le Duff M, Arnaldi B, Gouranton V, Jannin P. Training situational awareness for scrub nurses: Error recognition in a virtual operating room. Nurse Educ Pract 2021; 53: 103056.
[http://dx.doi.org/10.1016/j.nepr.2021.103056] [PMID: 33930750]

[11]   Georgieva D, Koleva G, Hristova I. Virtual technologies in the medical professions : Creation of 360 : Degree environments for health care training. TEM J 2021; 10: 1314-8.
[http://dx.doi.org/10.18421/TEM103-39]

[12]   Kleven NF, Prasolova-Førland E, Fominykh M, *et al.* Training nurses and educating the public using a virtual operating room with Oculus Rift. 2014 International Conference on Virtual Systems & Multimedia (VSMM),. 2014 pp.206-213.
[http://dx.doi.org/10.1109/VSMM.2014.7136687]

[13]   Al-Elq A. Simulation-based medical teaching and learning. J Family Community Med 2010; 17(1): 35-40.
[http://dx.doi.org/10.4103/1319-1683.68787] [PMID: 22022669]

[14]   Wittmann-Price R, Orrico S, Brogdon R, Morgan RD. Providing veterans with innovative nursing educational opportunities. Nurs Educ Perspect 2019; 40(6): E25-7.
[http://dx.doi.org/10.1097/01.NEP.0000000000000566] [PMID: 31644461]

[15]   Karataş Ç, Tüzer H. The effect of simulation-based training on the self-confidence and self-satisfaction of nursing students dealing with patients under isolation. Bezmialem Sci 2020; 8(3): 227-32.
[http://dx.doi.org/10.14235/bas.galenos.2019.3416]

[16]   Awad MS, Abdullah MK, Ibrahim RH, Abdulla RK. Nursing students' attitudes toward simulation technology in nursing education. Int J Emerg Technol Learn/ (iJET) 2019; 14(14): 31-45.
[http://dx.doi.org/10.3991/ijet.v14i14.10571]

[17]   Mickiewicz P, Gawęcki W, Gawłowska MB, Talar M, Węgrzyniak M, Wierzbicka M. The assessment

of virtual reality training in antromastoidectomy simulation. Virtual Real 2021; 25(4): 1113-21.
[http://dx.doi.org/10.1007/s10055-021-00516-3]

[18]   Rajeswaran P, Varghese J, Kumar P, Vozenilek J, Kesavadas T. Virtual reality trainer for endotracheal intubation. 2019 IEEE Conference on Virtual Reality and 3D User Interfaces (VR),. 2019. IEEE, 1345-1346.

[19]   Ho N, Wong PM, Chua M, Chui CK. Virtual reality training for assembly of hybrid medical devices. Multimedia Tools Appl 2018; 77(23): 30651-82.
[http://dx.doi.org/10.1007/s11042-018-6216-x]

[20]   Patel V, Aggarwal R, Osinibi E, Taylor D, Arora S, Darzi A. Operating room introduction for the novice. Am J Surg 2012; 203(2): 266-75.
[http://dx.doi.org/10.1016/j.amjsurg.2011.03.003] [PMID: 21703594]

[21]   Abelson JS, Silverman E, Banfelder J, Naides A, Costa R, Dakin G. Virtual operating room for team training in surgery. Am J Surg 2015; 210(3): 585-90.
[http://dx.doi.org/10.1016/j.amjsurg.2015.01.024] [PMID: 26054660]

[22]   Schild J, Misztal S, Roth B, *et al.* Applying multi-user virtual reality to collaborative medical training. 2018 IEEE Conference on Virtual Reality and 3D User Interfaces (VR),. 2018. IEEE, 775-776.

[23]   De Ponti R, Marazzato J, Maresca AM, Rovera F, Carcano G, Ferrario MM. Pre-graduation medical training including virtual reality during COVID-19 pandemic: A report on students' perception. BMC Med Educ 2020; 20(1): 332.
[http://dx.doi.org/10.1186/s12909-020-02245-8] [PMID: 32977781]

[24]   Frost J, Delaney L, Fitzgerald R. Exploring the application of mixed reality in Nurse education. BMJ Simul Technol Enhanc Learn 2020; 6(4): 214-9.
[http://dx.doi.org/10.1136/bmjstel-2019-000464] [PMID: 35520006]

[25]   Davis FD, Bagozzi RP, Warshaw PR. User acceptance of computer technology: A comparison of two theoretical models. Manage Sci 1989; 35(8): 982-1003.
[http://dx.doi.org/10.1287/mnsc.35.8.982]

[26]   Charness N, Boot WR. Technology, gaming, and social networking Handbook of the Psychology of Aging. Elsevier 2016.

[27]   Mathieson K. Predicting user intentions: Comparing the technology acceptance model with the theory of planned behavior. Inf Syst Res 1991; 2(3): 173-91.
[http://dx.doi.org/10.1287/isre.2.3.173]

[28]   Pintrich PR. The role of goal orientation in self-regulated learning Handbook of self-regulation. Elsevier 2000.

[29]   Huang H-M, Liaw S-S. An analysis of learners' intentions toward virtual reality learning based on constructivist and technology acceptance approaches. Int Rev Res Open Distrib Learn 2018; 19(1).

[30]   Hsu CC, Chen YL, Lin CY, Lien W. Cognitive development, self-efficacy, and wearable technology use in a virtual reality language learning environment: A structural equation modeling analysis. Curr Psychol 2022; 41(3): 1618-32.
[http://dx.doi.org/10.1007/s12144-021-02252-y]

[31]   Al-Azawei A, Baiee W R, Mohammed M A. Learners' experience towards e-assessment tools: A comparative study on virtual reality and moodle quiz. Int J Emerg Technol Learn (iJET) 2019; 14(5): 34-50.

[32]   Huang HM, Liaw SS, Lai CM. Exploring learner acceptance of the use of virtual reality in medical education: A case study of desktop and projection-based display systems. Interact Learn Environ 2016; 24(1): 3-19.
[http://dx.doi.org/10.1080/10494820.2013.817436]

[33]   Ali H, Ahmed AA, Tariq TG, Safdar H. Second Life (SL) in Education: The intensions to use at

university of bahrain. 2013 Fourth International Conference on e-Learning Best Practices in Management, Design and Development of e-Courses: Standards of Excellence and Creativity,. 2013. IEEE, 205-215.

[34]   Iqbal J, Sidhu MS. Acceptance of dance training system based on augmented reality and technology acceptance model (TAM). Virtual Real 2022; 26(1): 33-54.
[http://dx.doi.org/10.1007/s10055-021-00529-y]

[35]   Venkatesh V, Morris MG, Davis GB, Davis FD. User acceptance of information technology: Toward a unified view. Manage Inf Syst Q 2003; 27(3): 425-78.
[http://dx.doi.org/10.2307/30036540]

[36]   Bracq MS, Michinov E, Arnaldi B, *et al.* Learning procedural skills with a virtual reality simulator: An acceptability study. Nurse Educ Today 2019; 79: 153-60.
[http://dx.doi.org/10.1016/j.nedt.2019.05.026] [PMID: 31132727]

[37]   Shen C, Ho J, Ly PTM, Kuo T. Behavioural intentions of using virtual reality in learning: perspectives of acceptance of information technology and learning style. Virtual Real 2019; 23(3): 313-24.
[http://dx.doi.org/10.1007/s10055-018-0348-1]

[38]   Ajzen I, Fishbein M, Lohmann S, Albarracín D. The influence of attitudes on behavior. The handbook of attitudes 2018; pp. 197-255.

[39]   Ajzen I. Perceived behavioral control, self-efficacy, locus of control, and the theory of planned behavior 1. J Appl Soc Psychol 2002; 32(4): 665-83.
[http://dx.doi.org/10.1111/j.1559-1816.2002.tb00236.x]

[40]   Ryan S, Carr A. Applying the biopsychosocial model to the management of rheumatic disease Rheumatology. Elsevier 2010.

[41]   Fussell SG, Truong D. Using virtual reality for dynamic learning: An extended technology acceptance model. Virtual Real 2022; 26(1): 249-67.
[http://dx.doi.org/10.1007/s10055-021-00554-x] [PMID: 34276237]

[42]   Kwok PK, Yan M, Qu T, Lau HYK. User acceptance of virtual reality technology for practicing digital twin-based crisis management. Int J Comput Integrated Manuf 2021; 34(7-8): 874-87.
[http://dx.doi.org/10.1080/0951192X.2020.1803502]

[43]   Zhou M. Chinese university students' acceptance of MOOCs: A self-determination perspective. Comput Educ 2016; 92-93: 194-203.
[http://dx.doi.org/10.1016/j.compedu.2015.10.012]

[44]   Mouloudj K, Bouarar A C, Stojczew K. Analyzing the students' intention to use online learning system in the context of COVID-19 pandemic: A theory of planned behavior approach 2021.

[45]   Lee MC. Explaining and predicting users' continuance intention toward e-learning: An extension of the expectation–confirmation model. Comput Educ 2010; 54(2): 506-16.
[http://dx.doi.org/10.1016/j.compedu.2009.09.002]

[46]   Cheon J, Lee S, Crooks SM, Song J. An investigation of mobile learning readiness in higher education based on the theory of planned behavior. Comput Educ 2012; 59(3): 1054-64.
[http://dx.doi.org/10.1016/j.compedu.2012.04.015]

[47]   Tagoe MA, Abakah E. Determining distance education students' readiness for mobile learning at university of ghana using the theory of planned behavior. Int J Educ Dev Using Inf Commun Technol 2014; 10: 91-106.

[48]   Schepers J, Wetzels M. A meta-analysis of the technology acceptance model: Investigating subjective norm and moderation effects. Inf Manage 2007; 44(1): 90-103.
[http://dx.doi.org/10.1016/j.im.2006.10.007]

[49]   Lamorte WW. Behavioral change models: The theory of planned behavior. Retrieved 2019; (December): 20.

CHAPTER 2

Digital Health with Smart Internet of Things (IoT) Technologies

Abstract: Hospitals, nursing homes, and other healthcare facilities will face considerable problems in the next decades due to the aging population's increasing healthcare demands, the complexity of modern healthcare delivery, and the rising expectations of healthcare consumers. Future healthcare development must continue to face problems, which call for more digital innovation. One of the goals for the ensuing decades will be to craft a clever plan to advance digital health. The smart Internet of Things (IoT) technologies are crucial elements to integrate digital health for enabling practical utilization in the field, given the large range of information technologies available. The smart IoT supports medical practitioners in their working process and facilitates the management of the patient's health records. In this chapter, we explore some of the key smart IoT technologies in digital health and management including data acquisition, data transmission, and positioning. Each technology is briefly introduced to provide insights that will allow readers to adopt the essential technologies for potential future practical applications.

Keywords: Artificial intelligence, Big data, Cloud computing, Cyber-physical system, Internet of Things, Information system, Smart devices, 5G.

1. INTRODUCTION

With the wider adoption of a new generation of information technologies such as big data, cloud computing, industry 4.0, artificial intelligence, smart healthcare, and related concepts have gradually come to the fore. Digital health or digital healthcare is a broad and multidisciplinary concept that illustrates the integration of various latest digital technologies into healthcare applications. Although there are no unique definitions of smart healthcare, it usually refers to the adoption of the latest computer and information technologies to transform the traditional healthcare system and medical practices in an all-round way, in order to make healthcare service more efficient and effective, as well as enhancing the safety, reliability, and transparency of medical treatment and therapy processes. Digital health is essential and the adoption of the latest technologies is important to provide quality service to the community. The latest technologies include virtual reality (VR), the Internet of Things (IoT), artificial intelligence (AI), blockchain, smart devices, *etc.* These technologies can support digital health in various aspects. For instance, VR is widely used for training healthcare practitioners, as well as patients [1, 2], while AI can be used for supporting the segmentation of the CT or MRI for medical doctors to support the diagnosis, as well as the forecasting purposes [3 - 5]. Blockchain technology can be used to enhance traceability and trackability to enhance management in aviation and other industries [6]. Among all of these technologies, smart devices and IoT in contrast provide the essential infrastructure for sensing, communication, and identification to facilitate the logistics process. These fundamental technologies are essential for enhancing the efficiency, effectiveness, and smoothness of the logistics processes, as well as for improving management. The technologies are primarily used to serve the logistics industries, in fact, it has also been extended to a wide range of applications in the health and medical industries. The smart IoT supports medical practitioners in their working processes and facilitates the management of a patient's health records. The wide range of applications of smart IoTs is useful in digital healthcare and management.

We first review the key data acquisition technologies that are commonly used in smart and digital healthcare. Then, we also explore the key technologies for data transfer, as well as positioning. Data acquisition, transfer, and positioning technologies are essential in many practical applications and enable the practical implementation of smart healthcare and management applications. The data acquisition techniques can be used to obtain data, patients' behavior, and other information, and data transmission technology can be used to send data by wire or wireless means to the management platform. The monitoring management can use various algorithms such as AI and big data analytics to serve in several core fields of smart applications such as diagnosis, treatment, health management, preventive and risk management. The last section gives a brief conclusion to this chapter.

2. DATA ACQUISITION TECHNOLOGIES

Data acquisition is a method that typically employs smart devices, sensors, and Internet of Things (IoT) technologies to collect data from humans, machines, equipment, *etc.*, which is then used as input by an organization or internal systems. For instance, cameras and microphones are examples of common data-collecting instruments used in everyday life. The acquired data are typically physical quantities such as temperature, water level, wind speed, and pressure that are transformed into electrical signals. The data may be analog or digital, and the acquisition technology is often a sampling technique that repeatedly receives the data at the same spot at a predetermined sampling interval. The majority of the acquired data include immediate values, as well as values representative of a specific period. The state of the measured object and the measuring environment must be considered in order to guarantee the accuracy of the acquired data. Sensors are often contact-based data-collecting devices, whereas vision and radar are non-contact data-gathering technologies that are widely utilized nowadays. In the sections that follow, the specifics of the various data-collecting methods and how the technologies can be applied to digital health and management, such as human behavior recognition, are described.

2.1. Vision Approach

In recent years, with the widespread usage of video perception devices, including 2D and depth cameras, as well as the increasing performance of computing equipment and storage capacity, research, and applications based on computer vision technology have been steadily promoted [7]. On implementation of video sensors, such as human body motion detection, failure detection, surveillance, *etc*, vision data can be utilized to identify the body's action perception and behavior, while computer vision technology can be applied in the field of pattern recognition in digital healthcare for intelligent video surveillance, human-computer interaction, medical diagnosis, health monitoring, *etc.*

Numerous real-world applications that use an image-based method for subsequent processing depend on the application of visual technology for data collecting. Unlike other sensing devices, the video image acquisition device can be utilized in any area and under any circumstance. Nevertheless, the utilization of visual technology requires the creation of additional software systems and digital algorithms for data processing. For example, when a camera captures the movement of humans, the original image or image sequence will invariably include the surrounding environment. In this instance, the visual images or videos will depict the human body in the foreground and the surrounding environment in the backdrop. To distinguish the human body from the surrounding environment, image segmentation algorithms and other methods are necessary. Based on the image's dynamic properties, the vision-based image segmentation method can be separated into static segmentation and motion segmentation. Static segmentation has a pretty extensive history of research. There are representative approaches and methods that can be used, such as the edge detection-based segmentation method, the threshold-based segmentation method, the region-based segmentation method, and the wavelet transforms segmentation method. Since the fundamental characteristic of a moving image is the change in gray level, the dynamic image is segmented differently than the static image. Existing approaches can be categorized based on two factors: the characteristic of the moving image itself and the degree of artificial engagement.

2.2. Acceleration Sensors

Some applications in healthcare entail tracking humans, such as the possible safety behavior of patients, the tracking of medicines and other things, *etc.* The movement of the human body and objects is frequently followed by a change in acceleration information, regardless of whether the activity involves walking, jumping, waving, or swinging arms. Acceleration information may therefore be essential for determining the possible movement characteristics of the human body and other objects. Currently, behavior and motion recognition based on the analysis of acceleration signals are utilized extensively in energy consumption evaluation, intelligent monitoring, medical care, *etc* [8]. A sensor measures and converts acceleration signals into electrical signals.

Typically, the micro-acceleration sensor measures acceleration using a sensitive mass block. The external acceleration operates on the mass block; the acceleration value is then determined by measuring the displacement of the mass block, the force exerted by the mass block on the frame, or the force necessary to maintain its position [9]. There are numerous techniques for measuring force or displacement, including strain gauges, capacitance gauges, strain-sensitive resonant beams, tunnel detectors, surface acoustic devices, magnetometers, optical detectors, *etc.* Micro-acceleration sensors can be divided into piezoresistive micro-sensors, capacitive micro-sensors, resonant micro-sensors, servo micro-sensors, and tunnel-type micro-sensors based on their detecting methods.

2.3. Gyroscope Sensor

Conventional mechanical gyros measure the angular velocity of a high-speed rotating rotor by utilizing the conservation of angular momentum. The rotor rotates rapidly in a balanced frame connected by a flexible rod to the fixed frame. If there is an angular velocity input along the input axis, the rotor's torque causes the balancing box to twist in order to conserve the angular momentum. The angle of torsion can be measured by the sensor, and the measurement data can be retrieved by the peripheral servo circuit's processing. The rotor gyro is distinguished by its great precision, complex structure, short lifespan, and expensive cost [10].

A gyroscope sensor can measure angular velocity, and various object movements and human actions, such as turning the body, waving hands, turning the head, *etc.*, are followed by changes in angular velocity (Fig. **1**). By attaching a gyroscope sensor to an object or the human body, it is possible to acquire information that reflects the motion of the object.

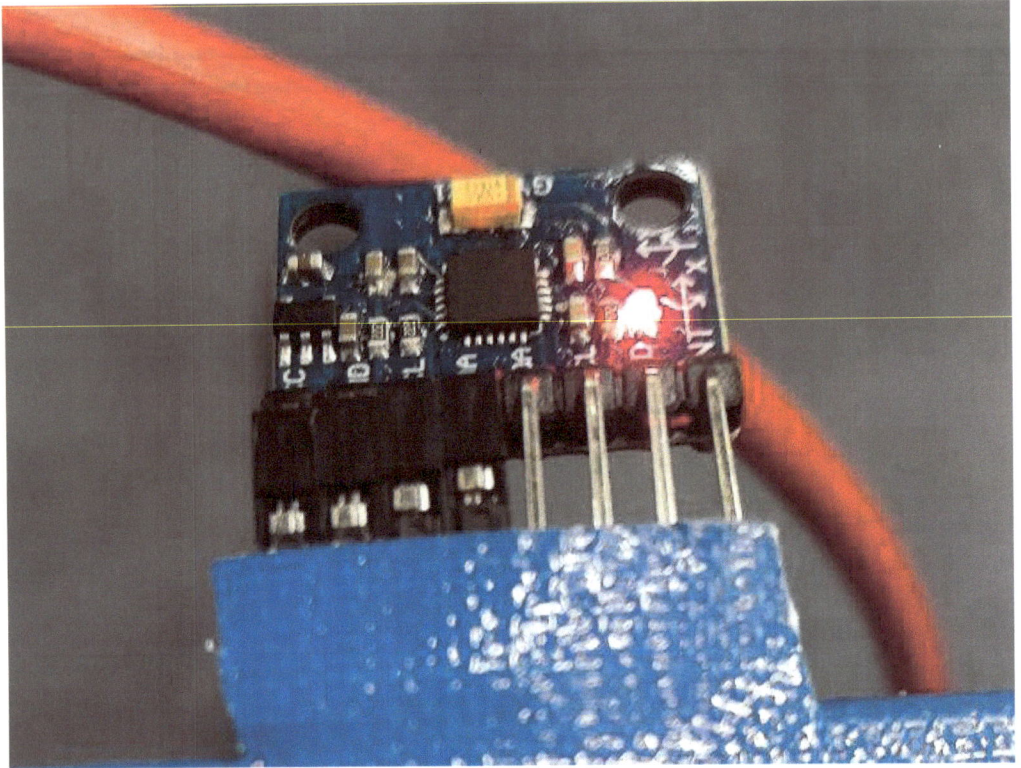

Fig. (1). Gyroscope sensor.

Due to the tremendous complexity of manufacturing a high-speed spinning rotor system, many gyroscopes now use micro-mechanical vibration gyros to measure angular velocity. Vibratory gyros operate based on the Coghlan effect, and the Coghlan acceleration is generated and measured by a certain type of device [11]. The Coriolis acceleration is proportional to the rotation speed of the rotating coordinate system. The trajectory of a ball going in a straight line from the center to the edge of a revolving plate is curved. The curvature of the curve is proportional to the rate of rotation, and from the top view, the ball accelerates significantly due to the Coriolis acceleration.

2.4. Radar Technology

Radar technology has been utilized in a variety of everyday applications for decades. The radar system, for instance, is used to detect aircraft in the sky. By analyzing radio signals, it determines the appearance, kind, and sequence of motion information of aircraft (*i.e.*, radio waves emitted by the radar returning to the radar antenna after being reflected by the aircraft or radio waves emitted by the aircraft). Recently, several researchers have explored and proposed ultra-wide Band (UWB) indoor radar perception technology suited to civic events, inspired by the military application of radar [12].

2.5. Summary

Each technique for data collection has its pros and cons. Unlike wearable technology, non-wearable technology does not require sensors to be attached for an extended amount of time and does not impose restrictions on the human body and other issues that could result in negative repercussions.

Non-wearable technologies, such as vision technology and radar technology, provide the advantage of collecting voluminous amounts of data with relative ease. Due to the vast quantity of information, some information may not be necessary. For data processing in this instance, a large-capacity storage device and computational power are necessary. Simultaneously, numerous image processing algorithms must be utilized to manage the data, posing a formidable obstacle for scientific researchers. Video surveillance is also likely to violate the user's right to privacy and safety.

Typically, sensor-based methods require direct or intimate touch with the actual sensor. The development of the micro-electro-mechanical system encourages the shrinking of sensors, reducing the influence of wearable devices on people's lives. Moreover, wearable devices are more sensitive to human activities and object motions, making them suited for motion data collection. In wearable technology, the acceleration sensor measures acceleration value; acceleration is the change in speed over time; therefore, when a person carrying an acceleration sensor device begins to change direction or speed value, he/she is able to detect acceleration; consequently, these sensors have become ideal sports equipment. The gyroscope sensor and acceleration sensor are distinct. The gyroscope can measure angular velocity, which is the change in angle position relative to time [13]. Due to the drift phenomena, the gyroscope occasionally accumulates errors, hence it is unsuitable for motion detection [14]. In conclusion, it is highly appropriate to apply the acceleration sensor in wearable technology to the collection of object motions, including medicine and medical equipment, as well as the behavioral data of the elderly.

3. DATA TRANSMISSION TECHNOLOGY

Data transmission technology is required for transmitting sensors, vision cameras, and radar data to the backend devices and systems. The two types of data transfer technologies are cable transmission and wireless transmission. The wireless transmission is comprised primarily of General Packet Radio Service (GPRS),

Bluetooth, Zigbee, and ultra-wideband technologies, whereas the cable transmission is comprised primarily of serial interface communication, field bus, *etc.* The following sections elaborate on the wireless transmission technologies covered in this chapter.

3.1. GPRS Technology

GPRS is a long-distance wireless communication technique that can provide a wide-area, end-to-end wireless connection. It offers data transmission at a medium rate by exploiting underutilized Time-division multiple access (TDMA) channels in the Global System for Mobile Communication (GSM) network [15].

The communication mode of the earliest fixed telephone network was fixed lines, which monopolized a fixed channel, as depicted in Fig. (**2**).

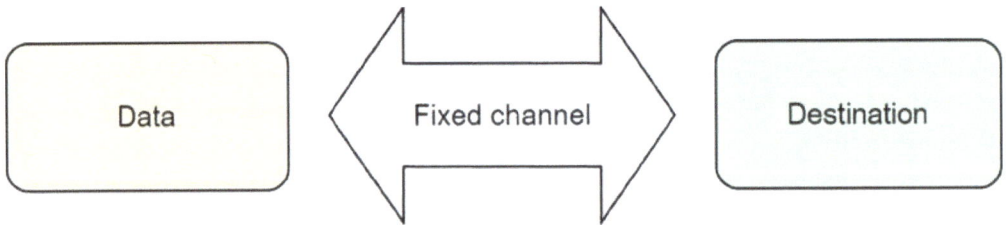

Fig. (2). Fixed channel mode.

As consumers' mobile communication service usage patterns change abruptly, the need for channel bandwidth fluctuates significantly. The GPRS protocol abandons the fixed channel in favor of packet switching. Fig. (**3**) depicts the schematic diagram of packet switching.

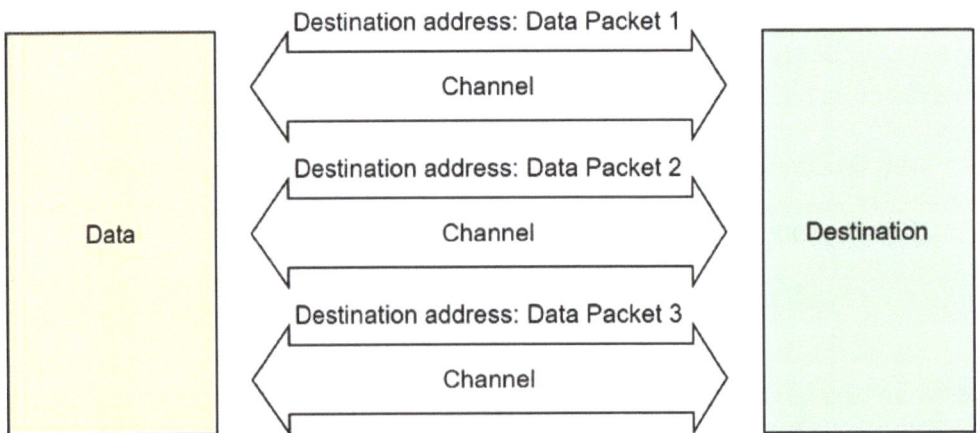

Fig. (3). Packet switching mode.

In this packet-switched communication mode, there is no need to allocate channels in preparation for data transmission. Instead, each packet's data header information is used to select a temporarily available channel resource to deliver the datagram (such as the destination address).

3.2. Bluetooth Technology

Bluetooth is a technique for short-range, low-cost wireless communication. Bluetooth's normal rate is 1Mbps, it operates in the 2.4 GHz band, and the transmission distance is typically 10m [16]. The Bluetooth system implements duplex transmission *via* a full-duplex time division (TDD) transmission technique. As illustrated in Fig. (**4**), the Bluetooth system consists of a wireless component, a link control component, a link management support component, and a master terminal interface.

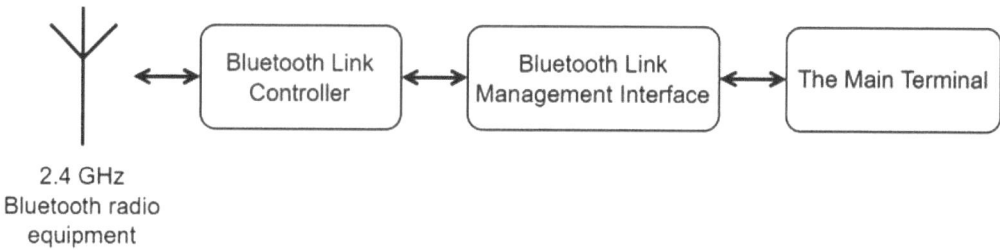

Fig. (4). Bluetooth system structure.

As illustrated in Fig. (**5**), the Bluetooth system's connection mode is divided into point-to-point connection mode and one-to-many connection mode.

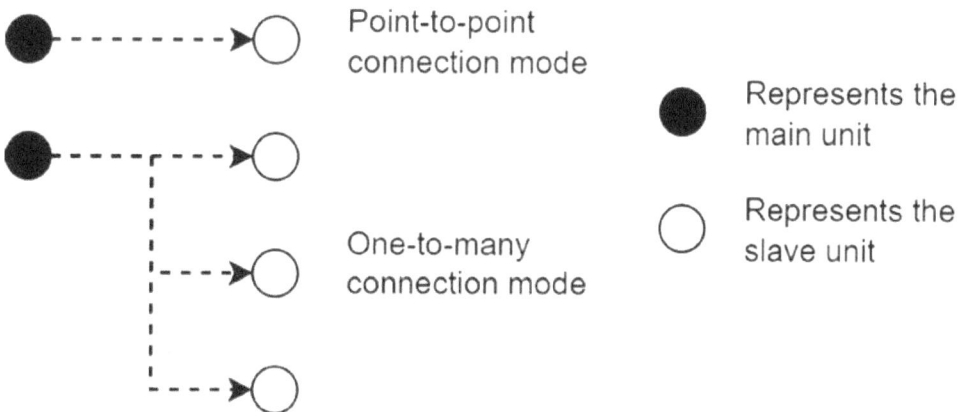

Fig. (5). Connection mode of bluetooth system.

Multiple Bluetooth units share a channel in a one-to-many connection, producing a pico network in which one Bluetooth unit acts as the master and the others as slaves. A network permits up to seven active slave cells and several inactive slave cells.

3.3. Zigbee Technology

ZigBee has proposed a type of close, low complexity and low power consumption, low data rate, and low cost two-way wireless communication technology, to support a large number of nodes, a variety of network topologies, and the speed, reliability, and safety of WSN communication [17], primarily for remote control, and is intended for components in inexpensive small wireless sensor networks.

ZigBee wireless communication technology is a network technology applied to Internet communication that is modeled around bee communication. In comparison to conventional network communication technology, the ZigBee wireless communication technology is more efficient and convenient. ZigBee wireless communication technology is a short-range, low-cost, low-power wireless network technology based on the IEEE 802 15.4 wireless standards for networking, security, and application software. This technology is ideally suited for businesses with low data volumes and may be implemented on a variety of fixed and mobile terminals. Additionally, ZigBee wireless communication technology can implement GPS functionality. ZigBee's topology consists of star networks, tree networks, and mesh networks. Here are the three investigated and analyzed topologies:

3.3.1. Star Network

Fig. (6) demonstrates that the stellate network is a radial network. In this structure, outlying nodes must be wirelessly connected directly to the central node. The greatest benefit of the network architecture is its simple structure, as it requires fewer protocols and cheaper equipment costs, and the central node performs the majority of the management work, hence decreasing the higher route's management burden. As a result of the need to position each terminal node within the communication range of the central node, the wireless network's coverage is inflexibly restricted.

3.3.2. The Tree-type Network

As illustrated in Fig. (7), a tree network is an example of a point-to-point network and a typical ZigBee network topology. In a generic point-to-point network, any two devices that can receive wireless signals from each other can interact directly;

no forwarding by other devices is required. Peer-to-peer networks still require a network coordinator, but its job is no longer to relay data to other devices; rather, it performs fundamental network management tasks such as device registration and access control.

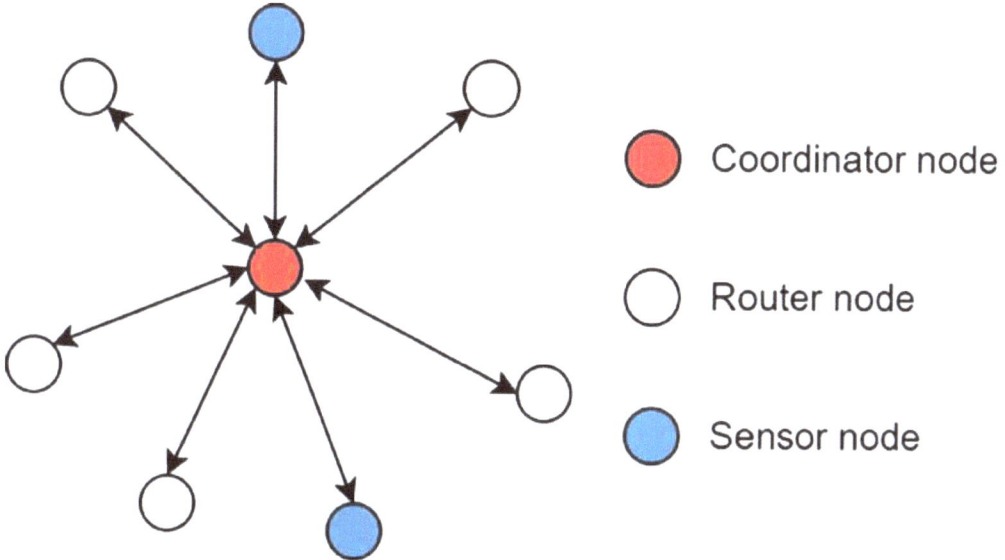

Fig. (6). Star network topology.

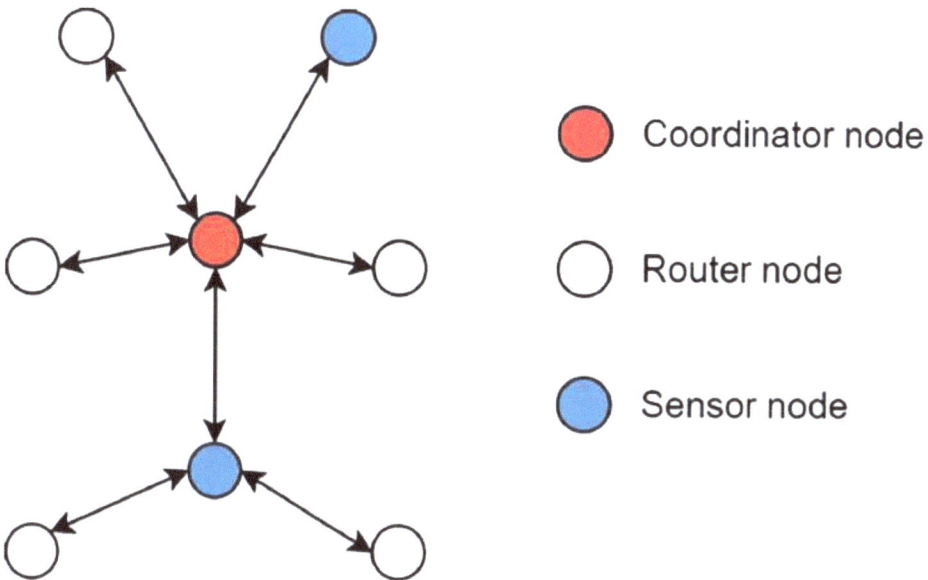

Fig. (7). Tree network topology.

3.3.3. Mesh Network

In comparison to the previous two network topologies, the mesh network has more robust capabilities. As depicted in Fig. (**8**), the network is capable of communicating across several hops. The topology can also comprise a highly complex network; the network has self-organizing and self-healing capabilities. A ZigBee network can include several routers but only one coordinator. The coordinator is responsible for establishing the complete network and can also serve as a communication hub for different types of networks.

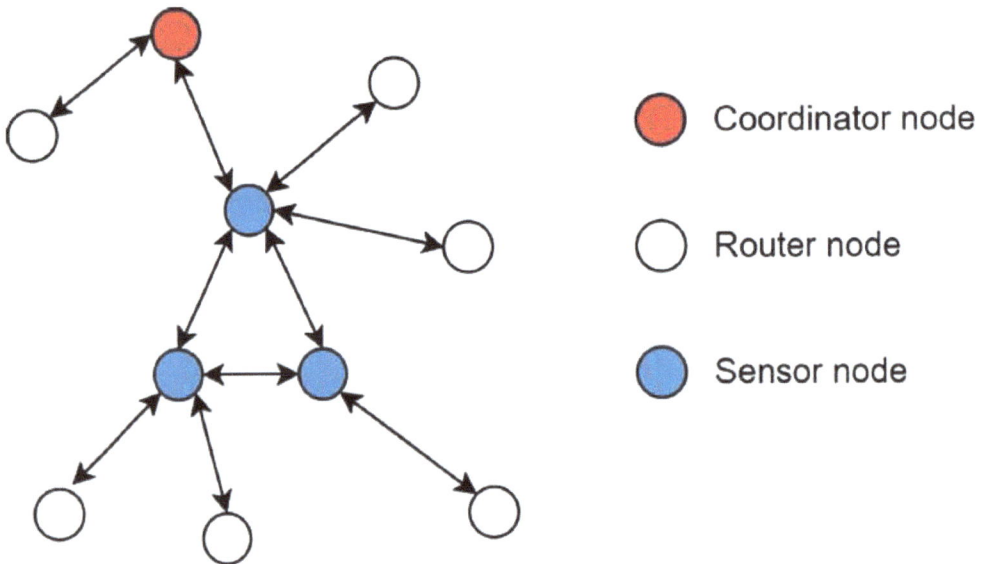

Fig. (8). Mesh network topology.

The following are the benefits of ZigBee technology:

(1) Low data transfer rate:

ZigBee's working rate of 20 250KB/s satisfies low-rate data transmission application requirements.

(2) Low electricity consumption:

Because the working cycle is relatively brief and the sleep mode is appropriately implemented, the energy required to send and receive messages is decreased. In the low-power sleep mode, two No. 5 dry batteries can run a single node for six to twenty-four months, or even longer. This is ZigBee's greatest advantage.

(3) Low price:

Each chip costs approximately US$2 due to the low data transfer rate, simple protocol, drastically decreased cost and ZigBee's lack of contractual patent fees.

(4) Significant network capacity:

ZigBee utilizes a star-shaped, tree-shaped network structure in which a single master node manages several offspring. A single master node may supervise a maximum of 254 children. Simultaneously, the master node can be administered by the network nodes of the top layer, which can comprise a maximum of 65,535 nodes.

(5) Temporary delay:

ZigBee has a rapid rate of responsiveness. Typically, it takes 15 milliseconds to transition from sleep to work, and 30 milliseconds for nodes to connect to the network. Bluetooth requires 3-10 seconds whereas Wi-Fi requires 3 seconds.

(6) Limited effective distance:

The transmission range between nearby Zigbee nodes is typically between 10 and 100 meters, and it can be increased to 1 to 3 kilometers by boosting the transmitting power, which is passed through the router node.

3.4. UWB Technology

Ultra-Wide Band (UWB) employs tiny, non-sinusoidal pulses to transfer data across a broad spectrum and is suited for short-range, high-speed wireless communications. In addition, it has other benefits, such as a high transmission rate, a big space capacity, good coexistence, confidentiality, *etc.*, which enables it to demonstrate better performance in radar, communication, and military applications [18].

New technologies and system solutions have emerged since 2002, including THE UWB system based on direct-expansion code division Multiple Access (DS-CDMA), the UWB system based on multi-band Orthogonal frequency division Multiplexing (MB-OFDM), and the multi-band pulse radio Ultra-Wideband (IR-UWB) system based on a carrier wave. UWB technology is currently the most competitive physical layer technology for short-range, high-speed wireless connections. IEEE has incorporated UWB technology into its IEEE802 family of wireless standards and is accelerating the development of the high-speed wireless individual domain Network (WPAN) standard BASED on UWB technology IEEE 802.15.3A and the low-speed wireless PERSONAL LAN standard IEEE

802.15.4a. UWB may become the dominant technology in short-range wireless networks such as wireless sensor networks, wireless personal LAN, and wireless home networks within the next few years [19].

3.5. Fieldbus Technology

Field Bus or the scene network was established in the early 1990s and promoted gradually in factories as one of the foundations of a digital communication network that can be utilized for process automation, manufacturing automation, and building automation. The field bus is also utilized in a variety of other intelligent device domains, such as intelligent instrument/meter, controller, execute equipment, *etc.*, and control connectivity between interior monitoring machines, in order to achieve two-way, serial, multipoint digital communication [20].

Fig. **(9)** depicts the conventional industrial connection type (a). Each item is individually connected to the control room, resulting in a complex installation circuit that is difficult to maintain and scale. If the control room is located distant from the plant, the cost of the control line cannot be disregarded. After employing field bus technology see Fig. **(9b)**, the large distance between the control room and the workshop requires just the installation of a cable, whereas the internal workshop is based on the bus, and all types of devices only require a short distance connection.

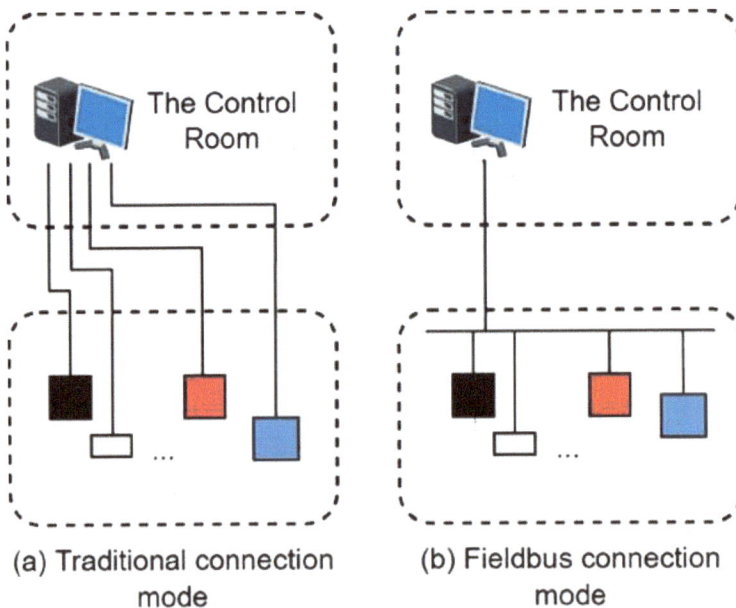

(a) Traditional connection mode

(b) Fieldbus connection mode

Fig. (9). Changes in industrial connection mode.

The introduction of Fieldbus technology represents a significant advancement since it greatly simplifies the wiring of communication and enhances maintainability and scalability. The initial terminal network is upgraded from a single-wire connection mode to a control room for a true network. There are currently around 40 Field buses around the globe, with the most popular being Foundation Field Bus (FF), Controller Area Network (CAN), LonWorks, DeviceNet, Profibus, Highway Addressable Remote HART, and CC-Link.

3.6. Summary

After the data are collected using an acceleration sensor, the sensor nodes must transmit the data to the monitoring platform. The data transmission process can be divided into two steps: the first step is for the sensor nodes to transmit data to the coordinator node. As a result, sensor nodes must be worn by the elderly in order to collect data on their behavior, and in a nursing home with a large area and a large number of elderly residents, data transmission can only occur wirelessly. Step two involves the coordinator node transmitting data to the monitoring platform. Since only one coordinator node is required and it may be permanently installed near the monitoring platform, cable communication technology is preferable to wireless communication technology due to its simple, safe, and cost-effective technology.

Considering that medical and healthcare application environments are typically hospitals and nursing homes, the transmission technology should possess the following: Low power consumption, small transmission distance (10 m to 100 m), minimal transfer rate (100-500 KBPS), low latency, and inexpensive networking. Comparing the above three types of wireless communication technology, GPRS is a long-distance wireless communication technology with a high latency that typically reaches 2 seconds, UWB technology is a type of short-distance wireless communication technology with a high transfer rate that can reach more than 480 MBPS and a transmission distance of fewer than 10 meters, and Bluetooth meets the requirements for low power consumption, low rate, and low cost, but its transmission distance is limited to less than 10 meters. Zigbee's transmission is typically used in an interior environment since its transmission range is greater than that of Bluetooth (10m-100m) and it is capable of large-scale networking [21]. Zigbee is ideally suited for the transmission of data in an interior environment due to its low cost, a little delay, and low power consumption. And in the selection of network mode, taking into account that the hospital and nursing home environment is complex, has a larger area, and more obstacles, routing nodes can be used to provide multiple hops paths for sensor nodes, so that the ZigBee network effectively covers the entire environment and ensures the stability of data transmission.

4. POSITIONING TECHNOLOGY

Positioning is another important digital health application technology. In a hospital or nursing home setting, the technology can be used to track the whereabouts of equipment and devices, medication, the human body, and other information. Commonly used positioning algorithms for wireless sensor networks fall into two categories: ranging location algorithms and non-ranging location algorithms. The approaches are described in detail below.

4.1. Range-based Approach

The ranging-based location technology mostly uses a three-sided measuring method and a multilateral measurement method, and the ranging technology primarily indicates arrival time, arrival time difference, arrival angle, and received signal intensity.

4.1.1. Distance Measurement Algorithm

The algorithm for measuring distance comprises the time and angle of arrival, three-sided measurement, and multilateral measurement technique.

4.1.1.1. Time and Angles of Arrival

The Time of Arrival (ToA) algorithm for measuring distance employs signal propagation. Time and propagation rate are used to determine the distance between two signal ends [22], and the propagation rate of the signal is known. The one-way arrival time method measures the signal-sending time and arrival time difference, which necessitates a device for synchronizing the sender and receiver's clocks with great precision. In the two-way arrival time approached, only the sending device can measure the signal's round-trip time. The two-way arrival time method is simpler to implement since it does not require a device for synchronizing the transmitter and receiver's clocks with great precision. In order to use the Time Difference Of Arrival (TDOA) approach, the transmitting device must emit two signals at different rates [23]. Similar to the TOA approach, the receiver may ascertain its position. The sender and receiver are able to collect extremely precise measurements.

Determining the direction of signal transmission using an antenna array or microphone array to measure the Angle of Arrival is another method for location. The angle of Arrival (AoA) is the angle between the direction of signal propagation and the reference direction (azimuth). Angle positioning is accomplished using the receiver array.

4.1.1.2. Receive Signal of Strength Indication

The received Signal Strength Indicator (RSSI) decreases as the propagation distance increases, and the received signal strength method uses this fact to determine the distance [24]. A receiving signal strength indicator that may be used to measure the amplitude of an incoming radio signal is a standard feature of wireless devices. In free space, the RSSI decreases proportionally to the sender's distance squared.

4.1.1.3. Three-sided Measurement Method

If the distance between the point to be measured and three reference points with known positions can be calculated in a plane, the three reference points are utilized as the circle's center to compute the distance between the source and the reference point. Fig. (**10**) depicts the basis of the three-side positioning method: Positioning calculations require four reference points in three-dimensional space for a spherical intersection.

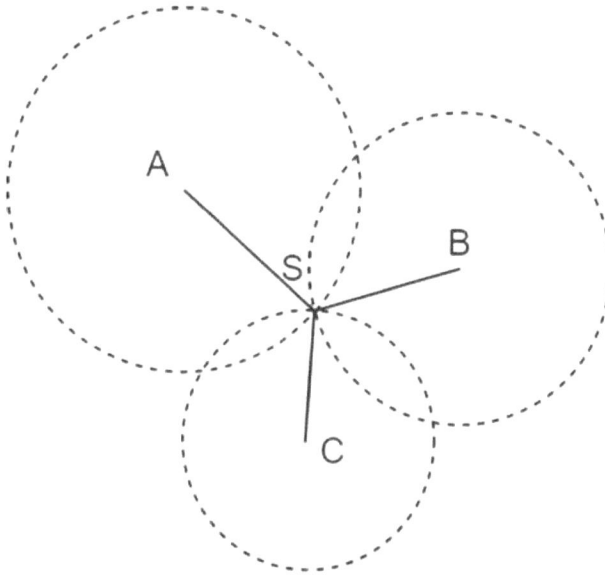

Fig. (10). Three-side positioning method.

4.1.1.4. Multilateral Measurement Method

The multi-lateral measurement approach can be utilized for positioning estimates when the distance between the positioning node and many reference nodes is measured simultaneously [25]. The concept is depicted in Fig. (**11**). The priority algorithm can be used to minimize the difference between the estimated and actual positions of the pending node S in order to estimate S's location.

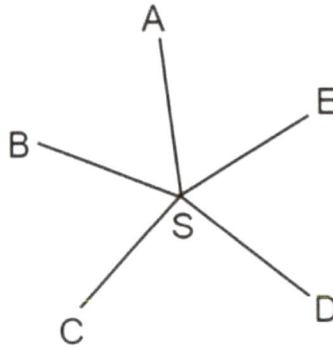

Fig. (11). Multilateral positioning method.

4.2. Non-ranging-based Approach

The location algorithm based on non-ranging does not require the ranging algorithm to estimate connection information rather than distance or angle. There are three primary positioning methods: centroid, triangle interior point approximate estimation, and DV-HOP.

4.2.1. Centroid Positioning Method

The centroid algorithm is a network connectivity-based outdoor positioning algorithm introduced by Nirupama Bulusu of the University of Southern California. The fundamental concept is founded on the geometry principle of the center of mass. As depicted in Fig. (12), the collection center of the polygons is known as the center of mass.

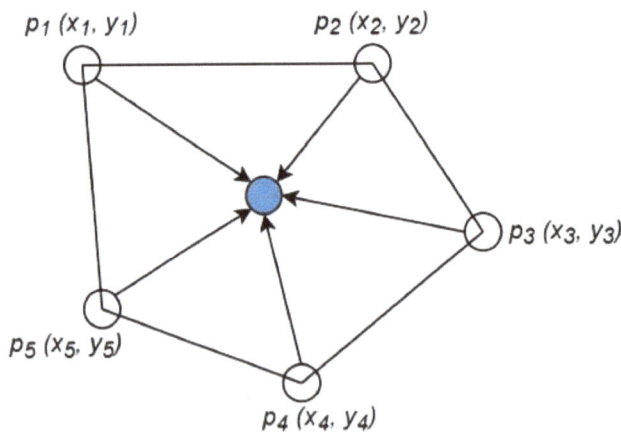

Fig. (12). Centroid positioning algorithm diagram.

4.2.2. Approximate Estimation Method of Triangular Interior Points

The approximate Point in Triangle (APIT) method determines the position of unknown nodes using the triangular region formed by anchor nodes. In the APIT algorithm, unknown nodes must first determine the location information of nearby anchor nodes before selecting any three to create a triangle. Assuming a total of N anchor nodes, c N3 distinct triangular regions can be identified, and each triangle is examined individually to see whether the unknown nodes are present. The position of unknown nodes can be found by calculating the center of mass of the overlapping polygon in all triangular sections containing unknown nodes [26].

4.2.3. DV-HOP Positioning Algorithm

The distance vector routing approach enables the unknown node to get the minimal Hop number between the anchor node and the unknown node; this is the fundamental concept of the DV-HOP placement algorithm [27]. When the unknown node acquires the position data of three or more anchor nodes, it uses fundamental techniques such as three-side measurement to estimate its position. The particular algorithm is illustrated in Fig. (**13**):

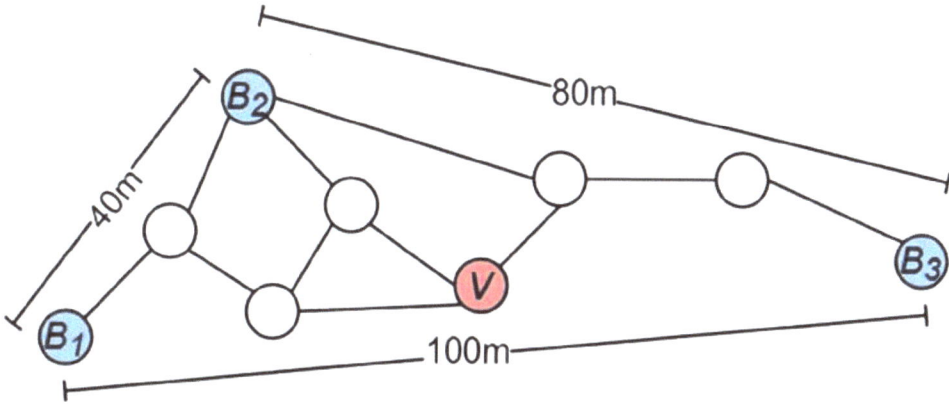

Fig. (13). Distance estimation of the dv-hop algorithm.

4.3. Comparison of Ranging and Positioning Technology

ToA technology requires time synchronization of all nodes in the whole WSN for the range algorithm, and the exact time of signal transmission must be known. In the meanwhile, processing latency and non-line-of-sight network propagation will result in errors. TDoA technology does not require knowledge of the signal's transmission timing but is susceptible to the effects of non-line-of-sight propagation issues. AoA technology necessitates that sensor nodes be outfitted with directional antennas or antenna arrays, which need an excessive amount of hardware and do not satisfy WSN's initial goals of low cost and low power consumption. This technique is a range-finding technology with low precision, but it is more suitable for WSN in comparison to the present trend of WSN device downsizing and low cost. This is because RSSI is susceptible to mistakes in various working settings.

The three-sided positioning method in the positioning algorithm is straightforward, however, it will not work if the three circles cannot intersect at a single place. Theoretically, the multilateral positioning approach can provide greater precision, but its processing cost is likewise larger, making its execution impractical. However, the density of reference nodes in the network has a substantial effect on the algorithm's precision. The greater the number of nodes, the greater the communication overhead and the greater the hardware needs. The DV-HOP positioning algorithm needs fewer anchor nodes and has modest computing and communication overhead but requires a high density of anchor nodes and can achieve a decent average distance per Hop in an isotropic dense network [28]. The centroid approach has minimal hardware requirements and is simple to implement in the software. However, in environments with a low reference node density, its positioning error is rather high. To obtain greater precision, additional reference nodes should be dispersed uniformly. In addition, the sensor node has limited on-chip resources, processing power, and battery capacity, making it unsuitable for employing complicated algorithms. Consequently, it is preferable to employ a centroid placement algorithm based on the specific situation.

CONCLUSION

This chapter briefly introduced the key techniques for the potential applications of digital health in hospitals, nursing homes, and other healthcare centers. The key applications of smart IoT technologies include monitoring and management of the elderly and patients, tracking the medication, equipment, and devices, *etc.* Indeed, all these applications require the essential fundamental technologies of data acquisition, transmission, and positioning. These technologies address the process of tracking, identification, and localization. Each variety of implementation schemes of key technology is described and the advantages and disadvantages of each scheme are compared. According to the characteristics of the technical scheme, particular approaches, algorithms, and devices can be selected for data collection, communication, and other purposes.

REFERENCES

[1]   Fong K N K, Tang Y M, Sie K, Yu A K H, Lo C C W, Ma Y W T. Task-specific virtual reality training on hemiparetic upper extremity in patients with stroke. Virtual Reality 2021; 26(2): 453-64.

[2]   Tang YM, Ho HL. 3D modeling and computer graphics in virtual reality.Mixed Reality and Three-Dimensional Computer Graphics. IntechOpen 2020.
        [http://dx.doi.org/10.5772/intechopen.91443]

[3]   Tang YM, Chau KY, Li W, Wan TW. Forecasting economic recession through share price in the logistics industry with artificial intelligence (AI). Computation 2020; 8(3): 70.
        [http://dx.doi.org/10.3390/computation8030070]

[4]   Li W, Tang YM, Yu KM, To S. SLC-GAN: An automated myocardial infarction detection model based on generative adversarial networks and convolutional neural networks with single-lead electrocardiogram synthesis. Inf Sci 2022; 589: 738-50.
        [http://dx.doi.org/10.1016/j.ins.2021.12.083]

[5]   Li W, Tang YM, Wang Z, Yu KM, To S. Atrous residual interconnected encoder to attention decoder framework for vertebrae segmentation *via* 3D volumetric CT images. Eng Appl Artif Intell 2022; 114: 105102.
        [http://dx.doi.org/10.1016/j.engappai.2022.105102]

[6]   Ho GTS, Tang YM, Tsang KY, Tang V, Chau KY. A blockchain-based system to enhance aircraft parts traceability and trackability for inventory management. Expert Syst Appl 2021; 179: 115101.
        [http://dx.doi.org/10.1016/j.eswa.2021.115101]

[7]   Masia B, Wetzstein G, Didyk P, Gutierrez D. A survey on computational displays: Pushing the boundaries of optics, computation, and perception. Comput Graph 2013; 37(8): 1012-38.
        [http://dx.doi.org/10.1016/j.cag.2013.10.003]

[8]   Quaid MAK, Jalal A. Wearable sensors based human behavioral pattern recognition using statistical features and reweighted genetic algorithm. Multimedia Tools Appl 2020; 79(9-10): 6061-83.
        [http://dx.doi.org/10.1007/s11042-019-08463-7]

[9]   Bezodis NE, Salo AIT, Trewartha G. Choice of sprint start performance measure affects the performance-based ranking within a group of sprinters: Which is the most appropriate measure? Sports Biomech 2010; 9(4): 258-69.
        [http://dx.doi.org/10.1080/14763141.2010.538713] [PMID: 21309300]

[10]   Zhang H, Zhang C, Chen J, Li A. A review of symmetric silicon mems gyroscope mode-matching technologies. Micromachines 2022; 13(8): 1255.
        [http://dx.doi.org/10.3390/mi13081255] [PMID: 36014175]

[11]   Dori G, Schliamser JE, Lichtenstein O, Anshelevich I, Flugelman MY. A novel system for continuous, real-time monitoring of heart motion signals. Eur J Med Res 2017; 22(1): 13.
        [http://dx.doi.org/10.1186/s40001-017-0252-2] [PMID: 28356163]

[12]   Shit RC, Sharma S, Puthal D, *et al.* Ubiquitous localization (UbiLoc): A survey and taxonomy on device free localization for smart world. IEEE Commun Surv Tutor 2019; 21(4): 3532-64.
        [http://dx.doi.org/10.1109/COMST.2019.2915923]

[13]   El-Gohary M, McNames J. Shoulder and elbow joint angle tracking with inertial sensors. IEEE Trans Biomed Eng 2012; 59(9): 2635-41.
        [http://dx.doi.org/10.1109/TBME.2012.2208750] [PMID: 22911538]

[14]   Shala U, Rodriguez A. Indoor positioning using sensor-fusion in android devices. Sweden: School of Health and Society Department Computer Science Kristianstad University SE-291 88 Kristianstad 2011.

[15]   Gamal S, Rihan M, Hussin S, Zaghloul A, Salem AA. Multiple access in cognitive radio networks: From orthogonal and non-orthogonal to rate-splitting. IEEE Access 2021; 9: 95569-84.
        [http://dx.doi.org/10.1109/ACCESS.2021.3095142]

[16]   Idris Y, Muhammad NA. A comparative study of wireless communication protocols: zigbee *vs.* bluetooth. Proceedings of the 33rd annual conference of the ieee industrial electronics society (IECON 2007), 2016.

[17]   Ramya CM, Shanmugaraj M, Prabakaran R. Study on ZigBee technology. 2011 3rd international conference on electronics computer technology, 2011. IEEE, 297-301.

[18]   Bin Obadi A, Soh PJ, Aldayel O, Al-Doori MH, Mercuri M, Schreurs D. A survey on vital signs detection using radar techniques and processing with FPGA implementation. IEEE Circuits Syst Mag 2021; 21(1): 41-74.
[http://dx.doi.org/10.1109/MCAS.2020.3027445]

[19]   Cao H, Leung V, Chow C, Chan H. Enabling technologies for wireless body area networks: A survey and outlook. IEEE Commun Mag 2009; 47(12): 84-93.
[http://dx.doi.org/10.1109/MCOM.2009.5350373]

[20]   Chen H, Jia X, Li H. A brief introduction to IoT gateway IET international conference on communication technology and application (ICCTA 2011). IET 2011; pp. 610-3.

[21]   Talla V, Smith J, Gollakota S. Advances and open problems in backscatter networking. GetMobile. Mobile Computing and Communications 2021; 24: 32-8.

[22]   Dong Q, Dargie W. Evaluation of the reliability of RSSI for indoor localization. 2012 International Conference on Wireless Communications in Underground and Confined Areas, 2012 pp.1-6.

[23]   El Moutia A, Makki K, Pissinou N. Tpls: A time and power based localization scheme for indoor WLAN using sensor networks. 2007 IEEE Conference on Technologies for Homeland Security 2007 pp.117-122.
[http://dx.doi.org/10.1109/THS.2007.370031]

[24]   Jianyong Z, Haiyong L, Zili C, Zhaohui L. Rssi based bluetooth low energy indoor positioning. 2014 International Conference on Indoor Positioning and Indoor Navigation (IPIN) 2014 pp.526-533.
[http://dx.doi.org/10.1109/IPIN.2014.7275525]

[25]   Shu T, Chen Y, Yang J, Williams A. Multi-lateral privacy-preserving localization in pervasive environments. IEEE INFOCOM 2014 - IEEE Conference on Computer Communications Toronto, ON, Canada, 2014, pp. 2319-2327.
[http://dx.doi.org/10.1109/INFOCOM.2014.6848176]

[26]   Demilew SA, Ejigu D, Da-Costa G, Pierson J-M. Novel reliable range-free geo-localization algorithm in wireless networks: Centre of the smallest communication overlap polygon (CSCOP). 2015 IEEE International Black Sea Conference on Communications and Networking (BlackSeaCom) 2015 pp.181-185.
[http://dx.doi.org/10.1109/BlackSeaCom.2015.7185111]

[27]   Han D, Wang J, Tang C, Weng TH, Li KC, Dobre C. A multi-objective distance vector-hop localization algorithm based on differential evolution quantum particle swarm optimization. Int J Commun Syst 2021; 34(14): e4924.
[http://dx.doi.org/10.1002/dac.4924]

[28]   Wan J, Guo X, Yu N, Wu Y, Feng R. Multi-hop localization algorithm based on grid-scanning for wireless sensor networks. Sensors 2011; 11(4): 3908-38.
[http://dx.doi.org/10.3390/s110403908] [PMID: 22163828]

CHAPTER 3

Human Remains Logistics

Abstract: Life and death are unique phenomena. Death is inevitable; thus, people will eventually become consumers of end-of-life products and services. The death care industry is currently facing radical challenges. The death-denying attitude can severely undermine the examination of the death care industry. Personal care and tailored informative services for the ultimate care of deceased loved ones must be given by a professional logistics service provider. The transport of human remains, bones and ashes requires professional knowledge of local regulations and laws, carrier rules and restrictions, rates and market demand, and shipment safety and protection, and communication between the carriers, customers and end-user (family members). On the side of the logistics service providers, they must overcome their fear of facing a dead body and address the funeral atmosphere of the workplace to improve their psychological well-being. This chapter includes five sections on the nature of human remains, specifications, human remains logistics operation, business ethics, and emerging market challenges of green burials.

Keywords: Business ethics, Death care industry, Human remains, Green burial, Logistics service provider.

1. INTRODUCTION

1.1. Funeral Logistics during the COVID-19 Pandemic in Hong Kong

The key issue of human remains logistics concerns sanitation and safety. Funeral workers were required to wear full-body protection suits during the COVID-19 pandemic (Fig. **1**). Since the outbreak of the new coronavirus at the start of 2020 and political issues and social movements in 2019, a large number of Hong Kong citizens have migrated to the United Kingdom, which increased the demand for human remains and related services between Hong Kong and the United Kingdom. During the pandemic, flight schedules decreased by nearly 3% to 5%, which created a high demand but low supply of cargo space. Thus, prices for cargo space increased by 500%–800% or more.

Families were unable to book flights to return to Hong Kong for the 21-day funeral arrangements because of not only the supply and demand problem but also the hotel quarantine policy. Thus, the bodies of deceased individuals remained in

Yui-yip Lau, Tang Yuk Ming & Leung Wai Keung Alan

mortuaries. For example, the author handled a case involving a body that was in mortuary storage for 180 days. In this case, the family members were very sad and anxious about the condition of the body of their loved one. Fig. (**2**) shows a simple funeral being held outside a public mortuary.

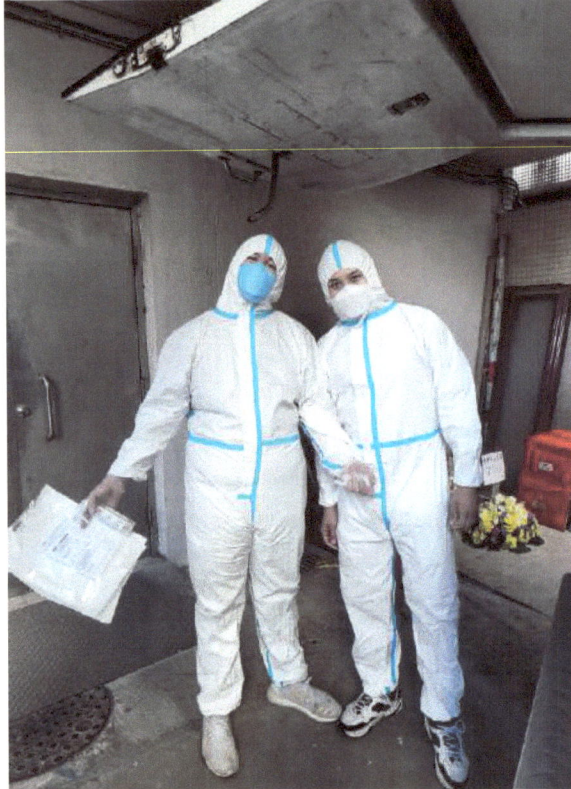

Fig. (1). Protection suit of funeral workers during covid-19 pandemic.

In case of migration, the process of relocating ancestors will follow, which can create business opportunities for the transport of ashes, remains, and bones. Finding a professional funeral transport service company in Hong Kong is difficult; thus, such services are generally entrusted to funeral undertakers. In addition, customers may encounter difficulties in overseas communication, because English is not commonly spoken by workers in the funeral industry. Hence, finding a company that specialises in funeral arrangements and transportation is difficult. A professional funeral logistics company must be able to provide 100% error-free service. The author has been working in the funeral logistics industry in Hong Kong and dealing with the global market such as the United States, Canada, China, the Philippines, Nepal, Australia, Ghana, and the Pacific Islands for more than 20 years. The author's company has handled more than 1,500 cases; thus, the author has valuable experience in the field. The problem particularly affects Muslims, because according to Islam, the burial of remains should be within 3 to 4 days after death. During the COVID-19 pandemic, in many cities under lockdown, waiting for flight schedules for more than one month was common. Such a situation is unacceptable and disrespectful to grieving families.

Fig. (2). Simple funeral held outside public mortuary.

2. AIR CARGO TRANSPORT OF HUMAN REMAINS

Being a professional means having a job that is respected, because it involves a high level of education and training. An individual with no training and skills to handle various types of problems cannot be called a 'professional'. Not everyone will be able to work in the funeral industry because of the gloomy atmosphere of the workplace. The work involves seeing sad and crying faces daily. Death typically does not induce feelings of happiness and relaxation. Coffins, urns, incense candles, shrouds, and corpse beds surround the funeral workplace. Moreover, funeral workers may be required to directly face, touch, and handle corpses to varying degrees. Some corpses are indistinguishable from living people in their sleep. However, some corpses are swollen, moldy, blackened, and seeping blood. In some cases, corpses may have maggots squirming on their faces or broken limbs. Such working conditions have frightened many 'ordinary people' from working in the funeral industry.

The air transport of human remains involves two professional services: air transport and funeral handling. Funeral logistics professionals must be knowledgeable and skilled in both types of services. From the transport and logistics aspects of human remains, processing documents and compliance with carrier regulations and government laws are important. Before processing documents, determining whether the deceased died naturally is necessary, because the transport of deceased individuals who died from unnatural causes must be approved by the court. The Birth and Death Registries under the Immigration Department are instructed to issue a body removal permit before a body can be transported out of Hong Kong. However, in the case of a natural death, such as an individual who died in a hospital, the situation would be simple. Families can apply directly to the Birth and Death Registries for a body removal permit without first applying to the court. In addition to processing documents, funeral logistics professionals must give accurate information on flight schedules and details. In many cases, customers will confirm flight times and dates to make funeral arrangements as soon as possible, such as reserving a mourning hall and hearse and making an appointment to collect the remains and other arrangements. The selection of a coffin, notification of family members and so on may be based on the scheduled departure time of a flight; therefore, information on flight details is essential. A slight error may set off a domino effect that will involve numerous people. Professional funeral transporters must have not only accurate flight information but also good relationships with and cooperative attitude towards airline personnel; otherwise, they may encounter difficulties.

In terms of transport, the port of origin and destination, size dimensions, weight, and commodity type are the most basic and important information. The world is divided into five oceans and seven continents; thus, being familiar with the geographical location of every country and town around the world is difficult. When handling customer inquiries, the ability to provide accurate and fast quotations and flight information is one of the skills of a professional. Hong Kong is home to hundreds of thousands of foreign domestic helpers. Based on the author's professional experience of more than 20 years and statistics, a foreign domestic helper passes away every week, on average, and must be sent back to their home country. In the case of Filipino domestic helpers, some may be from Manila or Cebu, but most are from small cities or villages. A professional must be able to provide the location of the nearest airport to the hometown to avoid wasting time and incurring unnecessary transportation costs. Professionals must also alleviate the anxiety and feelings of helplessness of family members.

In addition to the flight details and route arrangements, weight and size dimensions are important. A professional transportation logistics engineer must know the weight of the deceased, the size of the coffin, and the total weight of the cargo. To understand such aspects, one must first consider that a person may be fat in life but may lose substantial amounts of water and blood after death. The author once handled a special case in which they were informed that the deceased was a foreigner who weighed more than 100 kg. The prearranged measurement of the weight and size of the deceased would be impossible, as no guidelines exist for such matters. Hence, booking airline cargo space is difficult. A direct flight from one airport to another is not the only way to transport human remains; sometimes, transit in one or more airports may occur. Flights with transit stops can complicate a situation. International airports, such as Heathrow, Hong Kong and New York, provide world-class facilities and runways for all types of aircraft. However, some domestic airports, such as Saiya Airport and Hanan Island in South China, provide limited service and only to certain types of small aircraft, such as a B737 or smaller. Wide-body carriers such as a B747, an A300, a B777, and an A330 are not permitted to land in such airports. Moreover, the bulk hold space of small aircraft is limited and cannot accommodate cargo with a length of more than 180 cm. In other words, a standard casket for human remains will not be accepted by such aircraft. A professional funeral logistics personnel must be able to handle cargo space and transit schedule problems.

Dealing with the aforementioned problems is difficult for new staff with little experience. To complete an aircraft cargo space booking, the weight of the cargo must be estimated accurately based on experience. In some cases, families buy large (mainly Chinese-style) caskets weighing 130 kg, but in other cases, caskets may weigh 800 kg or more. The reason behind the large difference in weight is the factors affecting the weight of the cargo, that is, the type of the coffin rather than the weight of the corpse. Western-style coffins are generally used, as Chinese-style coffins are heavier and more rigid. However, Chinese-style caskets may provide considerable protection for the body and prevent it from decomposing quickly.

During the COVID-19 pandemic from 2020 to 2022, some wealthy families hired a private jet for human remains transport. In the early days of the pandemic, many countries implemented strong lockdown policies, and airlines refused to accept bookings. In one special case, in 2020, a family paid USD 150,00.00 to hire a private jet to transport human remains.

Packaging is one of the most important elements of safe transport (Fig. **3**). Many airlines accept human remains, bones, and ashes for air transport for not only commercial but also humanitarian reasons. Also, the human remains logistics firm needs to comply with certain aviation logistics requirements, customs, and local government regulations. However, a few airlines do not transport human remains for various reasons, such as lack of knowledge of or unwillingness to handle complicated procedures, use of a certain type of aircraft, or negative past experiences.

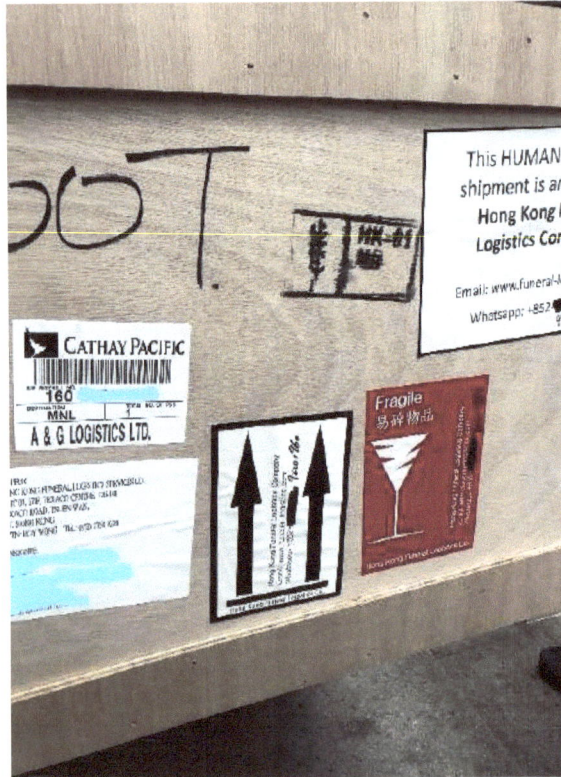

Fig. (3). Well-packed coffin for airfreight logistics.

3. EMBALMMENT

Embalmment involves temporarily preserving a body and improving its condition and presentation for funeral viewing. Embalmment applies to only burial cases (not to cremation funeral cases) and is performed to prevent the body from decomposing or to delay decomposition for at least 30 days. This chapter does not cover permanent decomposition, because the book is mainly about funeral logistics, human remains logistics, and compliance with airline and government regulations.

3.1. How to Perform Embalmment

Before embalming, the specialist must assess the condition of the deceased and determine whether it is suitable for the procedure because in some cases, the deceased body has decayed or moldered. Many factors may cause a body to decay, such as suicide by hand or burning charcoal in a closed space. In most suicide cases, the deceased was found after a certain time after death. Based on the author's experience in case handling, the longest time before a body was found after the suicide was 15 days. In this case, the body was black in colour, and the muscles had been dissolved, covered only by thin skin attached to the bones. In the case of drowning, oedema or dropsy may occur. When a funeral worker picks up a body with their bare hands, that is, without the aid of a stretcher, the skin may splinter from one end to the other. In a particular case, the author observed a funeral worker or deceased picker removing a body from the sea, whose muscles and skin had fallen off, exposing the bones. Besides assessing the condition of the body, getting formal permission from the government and official authorisation from the family is an essential step for embalmers to prevent any legal action from either or both parties. This step is essential in all cases, but especially in criminal cases. A death certificate will generally provide important information on the deceased, but a police report and/or coroner's court delivery order and body removal permit may also be used for verification.

In terms of the embalmment process, firstly, the deceased body is placed on a mortuary table in a natural position or supine anatomical position in medical terms. Fig. (**4**) shows a decreased body in transit from a mortuary to a funeral hall. Secondly, the body tags, in RFID form and written form, are checked simultaneously. Thirdly, the specialist inventories all the metal materials and personal effects on the body, such as rings and jewelry. The deceased body must be naked and examined for any damages. To give the deceased body dignity and pay respects to the family, the genitalia are covered with a white cloth. This practice is also a type of business ethics.

Fourthly, after completing the steps in the checklist and preparation, the embalming specialist uses sanitisers and clear water to clean the body carefully, especially all sutures, the eyes, ears, mouth, and anus. Then, the specialist injects a preservative and chemical liquid into the deceased body before excision. Formaldehyde is the main substance in the chemical liquid, or embalming fluid, which is used to preserve the body and delay decomposition. Glutaraldehyde is used for medication and as a disinfectant, and methanol is a type of alcohol. The embalming fluid contains the three aforementioned chemical substances and water in a certain ratio, depending on the condition of the deceased body.

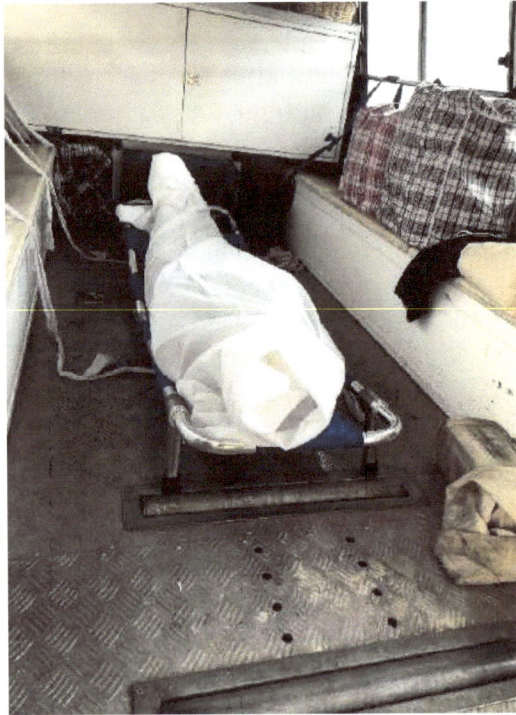

Fig. (4). Decreased body in transit from mortuary to funeral hall.

The last and the most important step in the embalming process is waiting for at least one hour to ensure that the body is presentable after the application of makeup and not leaking any fluids.

3.2. Meeting Airline Regulations

According to the International Air Transport Association (IATA) guidelines for all member airlines, human remains may be accepted for aviation transport under special requirement conditions but are not covered by the Dangerous Good Regulations. A dead human body may affect aircraft hygiene, such as spreading bacteria, viruses, fungi and mold to the passengers, crew, and any live animal onboard. A dead body may also stick to the surface of the cargo packaging, which may have a negative impact on the receiver and handling parties.

3.3. Meeting Government Laws and Regulations

Nearly every country has laws and regulations from its customs and health departments for hygiene control to prevent or stop the spread of viruses and/or bacteria from foreign countries. In most countries, a verified embalmment certificate is required for importing human remains. Embalmment is not a global practice, and most professional embalmment specialists have a background in anatomy, thanatology, and chemistry from medical school. In Hong Kong and in the United States, some medical facilities offer professional anatomy classes to those who want to become embalmment specialists. Such classes train students on how to use preserving materials drugs and embalming instruments.

4. BUSINESS ETHICS IN THE FUNERAL INDUSTRY

Sales in the funeral industry have commonalities with sales in the home furnishing industry. Sales contracts contain numerous professional terms. For instance, if you want to repaint your home, the brand name and colour of the paint will be mentioned in the sales contract, but who will paint your home, how long the paint job will be, and how to paint will not be included. Besides the sales contract, trust and the reputation of the company are important elements that also apply to funeral companies. A customer will have no opportunity to ask the funeral sales personnel to list all the funeral details in the sales contract, such as who will be the makeup artist, how will the body be dressed, what type of hearse will be used and how will the body be cleaned. If an error is noticed by a customer, making a request or filing a complaint would be difficult, out of respect for the deceased and because of the lack of details on the side of the sales personnel. In a particular case, a family paid a substantial amount for the funeral and high-quality casket of their loved one. When the casket was removed from a well-prepared metal case for overseas delivery, it sustained a deep scratch owing to the negligence of a funeral worker. The family members noticed the damage only at the funeral home but understood that expressing their anger would not make a difference. The funeral director did not reduce the price of the casket owing to their lack of business ethics, and the family members were unable to do anything about the situation. In another case, a customer was charged USD 200,000 for a unique wooden casket, and later learned from a family member that a different funeral home was selling the same type of casket for only half the price. The customer had paid a 50% deposit for the casket, but the funeral director would not give them a discount. The family had no choice but to accept the unbelievably high price of the casket and allowed the funeral home to handle the funeral arrangements.

The sale of unnecessary products is also a common misconduct in the industry. When a loved one passes away, family members will have very little time and will not be in the mood to compare services and goods before purchasing. In many cases, families realise that an all-in price is their best option. However, after a sale, funeral sales personnel may claim that some of the standard items may make the family lose face and encourage them to upgrade the materials or service. In the author's 25-year experience, in many cases, families are willing to pay more than 50% of the original price to honour their loved ones. In other words, in such cases, the funeral sales personnel will get an extra profit of 50%.

5. GREEN BURIALS

Environmental protection has become a hot global issue and trend. Green burials have garnered attention owing to decreasing forest land around the world. Environmental protection supporters believe that natural resources should be allocated to living people instead of those who have passed away. They also believe that embalming fluid is poisonous and harmful to the natural environment. Caskets and cement burials can damage the environment, because caskets are made of wood, and trees take a long time to grow. Green burial supporters propose the use of biodegradable caskets made from recycled material to return the deceased to the earth naturally [1]. They also suggest stopping the use of embalming fluid, which may damage the environment. The cremation of human remains can help conserve the planet's natural resources and land space. Green burial supporters also recommend other forms of burials that can help protect the environment and reduce the use of limited natural resources, such as sea cremation, tree cremation, and so on. Such burials would be greener and cheaper than traditional burials. Figs. (**5** and **6**) show examples of green burials.

Fig. (5). View of green burial grounds.

Fig. (6). Burial at sea.

CONCLUSION

To conclude, there are a few logistics firms that provide human remains logistics services in the world. Logistics firms encounter unfolded challenges to handle human remains during the COVID-19 pandemic. The lockdown policy, tight hygiene regulations, unpredictable freight rate, and a lack of labor further adversely impact the operational challenges. Besides, green burial may become a future trend in the funeral industry due to environmental concepts, government support, and limited land resources. As expected, the funeral operators may need to develop a new funeral service package focusing on green burial in the forthcoming years.

REFERENCE

[1]   Lau YY, Tang YM, Chan I, Ng AKY, Leung A. The deployment of virtual reality *(VR)* to promote green burial. Asia Pac J Health Manag 2020; 15(2): S53-60.
[http://dx.doi.org/10.24083/apjhm.v15i2.403]

CHAPTER 4

Building Resilient Vaccine Supply Chain during COVID-19 Crisis

Abstract: The COVID-19 pandemic occurred in the world in January 2020. Without specific vaccines and antiviral treatments, the virus easily spreads across different parts of the world. Accordance to the World Health Organization (WHO), COVID-19 has widely spread to nearly all countries across six geographical regions (*i.e.*, Western Pacific, Africa, Eastern Mediterranean, South-East Asia, Europe, and Americas). In doing so, different countries implemented various preventive measures like hand washing, lockdowns, social distancing, and mask-wearing to minimize the transmission of the virus. However, such preventive measures are short-term, ineffective, and may not be sustainable. The introduction of common vaccination campaigns is viewed as a vital effective way to against COVID-19. Over 60 vaccines for COVID-19 are either previously endorsed or going through clinical experiments. As expected, there will be an increasing need for people to accept vaccine injections. The vaccine is a highly vulnerable, high-value, and rare product in the world. As such, resilient vaccine supply chain management is urgently needed. Otherwise, the inferior quality of vaccines poses global health risks and causes the problem of wasting useful medical supplies. Nevertheless, some logistics firms encountered unfolded logistics challenges of the COVID-19 vaccine due to a lack of professionals, capacity, data integrity, inventory management, fluctuating demand, and geographic risk (*e.g.*, vibration, location, shock, and temperature). In particular, most logistics firms and health specialists encounter severe challenges in managing the vaccine supply chain in remote areas or developing countries. Although the vaccine is a global and hot issue for researchers, industrial practitioners, local communities, and policymakers, there is scanty attention to investigating the establishment of a resilience vaccine supply chain management in the context of COVID-19. At present, only a few research groups have discussed the role of blockchain in vaccine supply chain management, however, the information is not enough to reveal the impact on how vaccine supply chain management of blockchain can mitigate the COVID-19 crisis. Therefore, this chapter will mainly focus on the overview of the influenza pandemic around the globe, the existing situation of the COVID-19 pandemic in the world and Hong Kong, the current development of vaccines during the COVID-19 pandemic, the adoption of blockchain in the vaccine supply chain, and the vaccine logistics in COVID-19.

Keywords: Blockchain, The COVID-19 pandemic, Vaccines, Vaccine Logistics.

Yui-yip Lau, Tang Yuk Ming & Leung Wai Keung Alan

1. INTRODUCTION

1.1. The Overview of the Influenza Pandemic in the World

The first case of the 1918 influenza pandemic occurred in Spain, and it is also known as the mother of all pandemics. The reason is that the bacteria of the 1918 influenza virus were found in all subsequent influenza viruses. According to WHO data, the H1N1 flu in 1918-1920 years killed nearly 50 million people worldwide and infected one-third of the global population. Many viruses have the power of global infection. In particular, the influenza virus will spread and cause different species, including humans, islands, and pigs, which is characterized by the continuous spread in many countries.

Until now, the diseases related to H1N1 will combine with other influenza viruses and mutate, resulting in a new epidemic virus. In the 1990s, many severe influenza viruses were caused by human death and domestic avian influenza, including the Influenza A virus subtype H5N1 first discovered in 1997, and H7N9 and H10N8 viruses first reported in 2013. In typical years of seasonal outbreaks in the northern and southern hemispheres, there are as many as 5 million serious human diseases and nearly 500,000 deaths caused by influenza viruses [1].

The most influential epidemic in Hong Kong after the war was the first outbreak of new influenza H3N2 in July 1968, commonly known as the Hong Kong Flu. It is a kind of influenza A together with H5N1. Meanwhile, this virus is one of the epidemics with the highest death toll in history [2].

On February 22nd, 2003, the first case of Severe Acute Respiratory Syndrome (SARS) appeared in Hong Kong [3]. The virus is highly contagious, and there have been cases of infection and death in many Asian countries such as the Chinese, Taiwan, Hong Kong, and even Canada. The World Health Organization once declared Hong Kong as one of the "epidemic areas". It took four months to achieve zero infections and zero death.

From 2014 to 2016, the epidemic of Ebola Virus Disease (EVD) broke out in West Africa, and the whole world paid attention to it [4]. It was originally a fever virus discovered in 1976. Infected animals can spread their virus to others or animals and then spread it in the community by the human-to-human method. But the death rate of this outbreak is 50-90% higher and the side effects are higher. The worldwide popular viruses are summarized in Table **1**.

2. THE REVIEW OF THE COVID-19 PANDEMIC

On December 1, 2019, the first new case of human pneumonia appeared in Wuhan, China. COVID-19 was caused by (SARS-CoV-2) and the symptoms of patients generally included fever, general weakness, cough, sore throat, *etc.* However, a small number of confirmed cases had no symptoms at first [13]. On December 31, 2019, the Municipal Health Commission of Wuhan informed the public and the World Health Organization of a new pneumonia epidemic.

Table 1. Worldwide popular viruses.

Name	Transmission Route	Pandemic in History	Therapeutic Method
Yersinia pestis	Spread in the main rat population. After human infection, droplets produced through the respiratory tract spread through the air among people.	Causing the great plague of Justinian, the Black Death, and the third plague pandemic.	Up to now, there are very few cases, which can be cured with antibiotics.
Smallpox	The virus is transmitted through the nose, saliva, and fluid in the acne of the carrier.	At the height of the epidemic, 3 out of every 10 patients died, and smallpox claimed at least 350 million lives in history.	In 1796, a British medical scientist (Edward Jenner) developed the first smallpox vaccine.
Cholera	Acute diarrhea is caused by some pathogenic strains of Vibrio cholerae infecting the small intestine.	In the 19th century, there were seven global pandemics.	In 1893, Waldemar Mordechai Wolff Haffkine developed the first cholera vaccine. The oral cholera vaccine can have immunity for about half a year.
HIV/AIDS (human immunodeficiency virus)	Through body fluid transmission, attack the human immune system.	In 2016, WHO estimated that there were about 36.7 million HIV-infected people in the world.	Since 1981, there is still no cure.
Monkeypox	Direct infection through bites or scratches and spread by respiratory droplets.	The first was discovered in 1958 in monkeys kept for research. Mainly found in West Africa.	Jynneos Vaccine protects against monkeypox. The smallpox vaccine has proven effective against monkeypox.
Hong Kong Flu	Viruses are usually spread by droplets produced by coughing, sneezing, and talking.	About 1-4 million people around the world have died of influenza in Hong Kong.	In 1968, developed a vaccine against Hong Kong flu.

(Table 1) cont.....

Name	Transmission Route	Pandemic in History	Therapeutic Method
SARS	It is an airborne virus, which can be transmitted by small droplets of saliva, and its mode of transmission is similar to that of colds and flu.	There are about 8,000 cases of infection in the world, of which Hong Kong accounts for 15%.	There is no cure or vaccine.
EVD	It is transmitted to humans through close contact with the blood, secretions, organs, or other body fluids of infected animals.	As of October 2019, more than 3,000 cases have been recorded. The average fatality rate is about 50%.	There is no proven effective treatment for the time being.

Sources: About HIV [5]; CDC [6]; Cholera [7]; Department of Health [8]; Monkeypox [9]; Plague [10]; Severe acute respiratory syndrome (SARS) [11]; Smallpox [12]

In December 2019, many people in Wuhan, China, suffered from severe pneumonia, they thought they were infected by South China Seafood Wholesale Market so they suspended the place [14]. In January 2020, after an investigation, it was found that no one encountered the place and was infected with the virus, it was spread from person to person. At that time, it was the Chinese Lunar New Year, and many people went back and forth to their hometowns which caused the epidemic to spread on a large scale. Hence, the virus has spread to 34 provinces in China within one month [15]. Human-to-human transmission is mainly considered a respiratory tract infection caused by coughing or sneezing. Although COVID-19 first appeared in China, the virus evolved rapidly within four months and now it has spread worldwide. The World Health Organization officially named this infectious disease COVID-19 on February 11, 2020 [16].

As can be seen from Fig. (**1**), the number of COVID-19 infection cases in the world continues to rise from 2019 to now. Especially in Europe and the Americas, infection cases account for more than 70% of global cases.

As the number of confirmed cases and deaths continues to rise, COVID-19 has been defined as a global virus pandemic by WHO in March 2020 [15]. However, as of April 2020, the total number of infected people at that time was about 3 million, with about 200,000 deaths worldwide [17]. More than 210 countries and regions are affected by the virus, among which the United States has the most confirmed cases. Although China and India are among the most densely populated countries in the world, the local government immediately implemented effective blockade measures to control the infection of influenza. In October 2020, COVID-19 infected more than 36.5 million people worldwide and the death toll exceeded 1 million [18]. In March 2021, the number of COVID-19 cases in Europe continues to increase. Therefore, Europe re-adopted the measures of city closure and adopted stricter measures of social distance. Germany extended some city closures to April, Italy extended the state of emergency to March 30th, and Poland closed most public places for three weeks from March 17th. The French government even declared Paris and parts of northern France closed for four weeks. In June 2021, the cumulative number of reported cases in the world has now exceeded 180 million and the global death toll is close to 4 million. The Japanese government will donate an additional 2 million doses of the AstraZeneca vaccine to Taiwan Province and Vietnam, and another 1 million doses to Thailand, Malaysia, Indonesia, and the Philippines [19]. In March 2022, more than 455 million confirmed cases and more than 6 million deaths have been reported worldwide. France canceled most of the epidemic prevention measures, including showing vaccine passports in and out of different places and wearing masks indoors. Britain has lifted all anti-epidemic measures for outbound travel, and there is no need for any virus detection before and after entry.

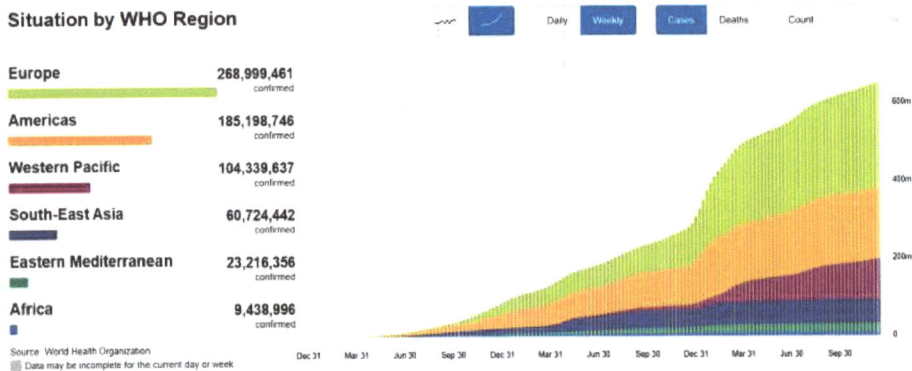

Fig. (1). Global covid-19 situation by world health organization (WHO) region.

Despite the progress of vaccination, the number of confirmed cases of the COVID-19 epidemic has been declining for more than a month, and the number of deaths and severe cases has also decreased. At the same time, a new mutant strain Omicron variant appeared. This virus is highly contagious, and the number of infected people decreased after reaching its peak in late January 2022, but it turned to an increasing trend again after March [20]. It accounts for more than 12% of the global infection cases in Southeast Asia, among which Hong Kong is the hardest hit. So far, the number of confirmed cases in the fifth wave of the epidemic has exceeded one million, and the number of infected deaths has reached nearly 7,000 people which also exceeds the total number reported by China. South Korea's recent single-day diagnosis is also the highest globally which shows that the epidemic situation is still very serious. The cumulative number of confirmed cases in Europe has exceeded 200 million, accounting for more than 40% of global infections.

COVID-19 has not completely disappeared and there is a new virus which is called Monkeypox. Monkeypox is caused by the monkeypox virus. It was first discovered in 1958 by monkeys used for research, mainly in Africa [9].

2.1. Impact on Social Activities

The epidemic has caused many countries to impose lockdown measures, and some industries have been forced to close, including beauty, bars, and amusement facilities. People's daily habits are beginning to change, such as reducing unnecessary recreational activities and maintaining social distancing. The purchasing power of consumers declines, which in turn affects the willingness of brands to place orders. Different industries need to adjust their operating models to adapt to the challenges.

As a result, many enterprises are working from home. It makes some retailers and restaurants have closed their shops or shortened their business hours, and some have even announced pay cuts or layoffs [21]. This has reduced sales in many industries. At the same time, under the regulation of the Hong Kong government, people need to receive vaccines before they can enter shopping malls or restaurants. This greatly affects the daily activities of people who are not vaccinated.

2.2. Impact on the Supply Chain

The face of sudden outbreak of the COVID-19 epidemic caused a serious disruption of the supply chain and led to a shortage of parts for some manufactured goods, especially in the automobile industry [22]. Because people suddenly need masks, disinfectants, *etc.*, the medical equipment and supplies needed to fight the epidemic are in short supply, which makes people think that the global value chain lacks sufficient response and flexibility when facing the impact.

The epidemic has hindered the frequency of shipping and air transportation, and the global shipping volume has dropped significantly, which has greatly increased the risk of default on the delivery date booked by overseas customers. It has also resulted in different problems such as production line shutdown, an insufficient supply of raw materials, and reduced orders in the supply chain. The COVID-19 outbreak can easily lead to inventory imbalances that are considered market failures, especially for companies with a Just-in-Time model and global production [23]. Thus, suppliers must re-plan goods procurement and logistics transportation networks carefully.

2.3. Impact on Tourism

The aviation industry is subject to international restrictions and suspensions, and it is expected that demand will shrink. Airlines and hotel companies have been hit the hardest. In particular, airline companies have significantly reduced their schedules, and some companies have already implemented unpaid leave [24]. In addition, consumers cannot travel because of this, and the turnover of some tourist attractions has declined.

At the same time, Hong Kong's economy has always benefited from a large number of mainland tourists coming to Hong Kong, which had a direct and positive impact on the retail, hotel, and catering industries. However, affected by the pandemic, the Hong Kong International Airport and the Hong Kong-Zhuha--Macao Bridge have to be closed, which greatly reduces the number of visitors to Hong Kong [25]. The business hours of shops have also been greatly reduced due to the restrictions on gathering, and the sales volume has dropped accordingly.

2.4. Impact on the Healthcare System

Before the outbreak of the epidemic, the original medical staff and resources in Hong Kong were already very tight. Due to the narrow living environment in Hong Kong, patients infected with COVID-19 are not suitable for treatment at home, so it is still necessary to increase isolation facilities to prevent the virus from being transmitted to their families [26]. Some citizens who have been tested quickly and found out that they may be infected with the virus will go to the hospital immediately, resulting in an overload of the medical system. Therefore, the government needs to immediately build isolation facilities for backup to solve this situation.

Different regions will allocate resources to track the virus. For example, to send enough manpower to each community to test the positive rate of testing for higher risk groups and symptomatic patients. Furthermore, the highly contagious nature of COVID-19 has led to a sharp increase in the number of community infections [27]. This has led to a substantial increase in the number of hospital visits, resulting in a sudden surge in demand for relevant medical staff, which has also increased the burden on the medical system.

3. EPIDEMIC SITUATION IN HONG KONG

In January 2020, Hong Kong identified the first case of COVID-19 infection. The first case of COVID-19 was reported on January 23, 2020. The government immediately closed several ports of entry and exit, such as the Hong Kong-Macao ferry terminal, but there were still different cases of local infection. Gradually different groups of infection cases continued.

In March 2020, the second wave of the epidemic broke out in Hong Kong. The epidemic situation in Europe suddenly worsened in March, causing many Hong Kong people to enter the country from abroad and then bring the virus into the community. At the same time, the Hong Kong Government has set up immigration restrictions, such as requiring overseas returnees to undergo compulsory quarantine for 14 days and imposing a "gathering restriction order".

In July 2020, the third wave of the epidemic broke out in Hong Kong. As the government agreed to the proposal of the Hong Kong Shipowners' Association to allow overseas seafarers and crew members to be exempted from quarantine, some infected seafarers landed and entered the community, increasing local infection cases. On 29 July, the government even imposed a full-day ban on dining in restaurants. However, the measure aroused public opposition, so it was canceled after only one day.

In November 2020, the fourth wave of the epidemic broke out in Hong Kong. On November 19th, a 75-year-old businesswoman brought the virus to the dance halls, causing a new round of community infection, with 50 more dancing groups. All restaurants and designated places need to apply for the government's "Safe Travel" QR code. All kindergartens in Hong Kong, primary one to primary three students began to suspend classes until December 6th.

In December 2021, the fifth wave of the epidemic broke out in Hong Kong. At that time, the government allowed Cathay Pacific to operate in the way of "passenger plane going and cargo plane coming back". Several cabin attendants failed to go home immediately after arriving in Hong Kong for self-isolation, which led to the arrival of the Omicron variant virus strain BA.1 subtype into the community. As a result, the number of local cases began to rise again. The epidemic continued until March 3rd, 2022 when the highest positive cases were recorded, and 76,991 cases were detected by rapid antigen test and nucleic acid test. On March 15th, 2022, a total of 3.58 million people were infected, accounting for nearly half of the population of Hong Kong. On April 9th, it had dropped to about 2,000 cases. Therefore, the government began to relax the social distance restriction in May.

The timeline of the COVID-19 epidemic wave is summarized in Fig. (**2**). The third stage of vaccine development is shown in Fig. (**3**).

Based on Lam *et al.* [28], there are different variant cases in Hong Kong, as follows:

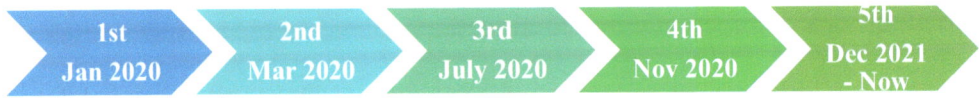

Fig. (2). The COVID-19 Epidemic Wave Timeline.

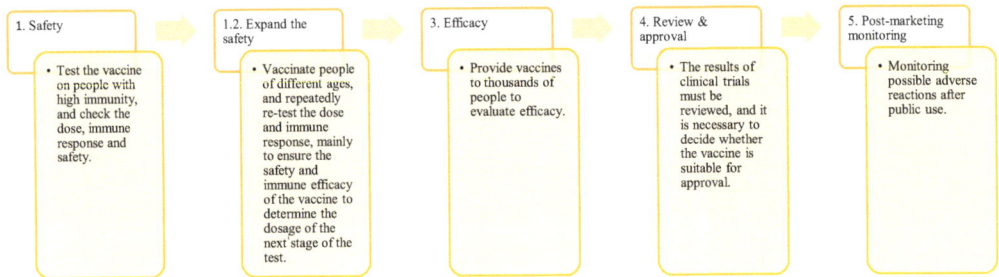

Fig. (3). The Third Stage of Vaccine Development.

● From December 2020 to February 2021, the first wave of Alpha mutation cases in Hong Kong, mainly imported from the UK, then rose briefly in May, mainly from the Philippines, Pakistan, and India.

● In early February 2021, there were cases of Beta variation, mainly from Philippine passengers from February to May 2021.

● In late March 2021, there were Delta mutation cases, mainly imported from India and Nepal.

● In mid-April 2021, there were Kappa variant cases, mainly imported from India.

4. THE HISTORY AND DEVELOPMENT OF A VACCINE

In the history of vaccines, it includes inactivated whole virus of vaccine, the attentive virus which is less toxic but still immune, or parts or subunits of the virus [29]. In the 19th century, the mystery of microorganism and bacteria theory was discovered through scientific research. In the middle of the 20th century, the first-generation vaccine in history was developed and known as recombinant DNA and whole-genome sequencing techniques were major components of the vaccine [30]. After years of medical research and technical development, then, a series of important vaccines were developed, including vaccines for Measles, Mumps, Rubella, and Varicella vaccines. The knowledge system of vaccines is constantly growing which is helpful to cope with future epidemics.

There are three main stages in vaccine development. The first stage is exploration, using different research calculation models to determine the antigen body and components of the vaccine. The second stage is preclinical research, using cultured cells and animals to conduct experiments to evaluate the safety and immunity of the vaccine. After the indexes are verified on animals, human trials will be conducted, and the third stage will be a large group test [31]. The third stage has five important processes as below:

4.1. Vaccine in COVID-19

In mid-2020, the global SARS-CoV-2 vaccine included 158 vaccines, of which 135 were in the preclinical or development trial stage [32]. The Food and Drug Administration has approved the use of Pfizer/BioNTech and Moderna COVID-19 vaccines in immunization programs. Pfizer/BioNTech recruited 43,661 participants and Moderna recruited 30,000 participants in the third clinical trial. The experimental results show that the vaccine can protect recipients and reduce the COVID-19 infection rate by forming antibodies and providing immunity against the COVID-19 virus [33]. Britain was the first country to carry out an immunization program. Pfizer & Moderna is a new technology with mRNA as an active substance and the vaccine contains RNA which is for cells to produce protein as an antigen [34]. Other vaccines use different types of antigens, such as viral vectors, attenuated viruses, and inactivated viruses. Sinovac is developing an inactivated and aluminum adjuvant vaccine [31].

In December 2020, the first COVID-19 vaccine jointly developed by Pfizer and BioNTech was approved [30]. As COVID-19 vaccine development is regarded as one of the fastest developments in the history of vaccine science, people are worried that the vaccine has not been effectively immunized against viruses due to its hasty development. It may lead to people losing confidence in the vaccine, so some people in various places have not been vaccinated. The COVID-19 vaccine are summarized in Table **2**.

Table 2. Summary of covid-19 vaccine.

Disease Agent	Year Identified	Vaccine Name	Year Licensed (FDA)	Vaccine Type	Route of Administration
COVID-19*	2019	Pfizer-BioNTech	Dec 20	mRNA vaccine	IM
-	-	AstraZeneca/Oxford	Feb 21	Adenovirus vector	IM
-	-	Covishield	Feb 21	Adenovirus vector	IM
-	-	Johnson & Johnson	Mar 21	Adenovirus vector	IM
-	-	Moderna	Apr 21	mRNA vaccine	IM

(Table 2) cont.....

Disease Agent	Year Identified	Vaccine Name	Year Licensed (FDA)	Vaccine Type	Route of Administration
-	-	Sinopharm-BBIBP	May 21	Inactivated	IM
-	-	CoronaVac	Jun 21	Inactivated	IM

Sources: Saleh *et al.* [30]

Table **3** shows that most governments prefer to give some financial incentives to attract people to get a vaccination in Asian countries. The financial incentives are given as a prize of lottery, homeware, or voucher. Some special incentives are also used, just as showing vaccine safety by government officials, and exemption fines. On the other hand, most of the government chooses to control the activity area to make people get vaccination, especially in Singapore. For example, if people do not get a vaccination, most of the entertainment venues, including bars and libraries, are not allowed to enter. In Singapore, unvaccinated people even cannot go to the workplace despite the inconvenience in daily life, people choose to take the vaccination. However, in Japan, the government thinks getting a vaccination or not should be decided by the willingness of the citizens. Therefore, there are no punishments in Japan.

Table 3. The Country Adopts the Vaccine Measure in Incentives and Penalties.

Country/City	Incentive	Penalty
India	• Free homeware to attract lower-class residents to get the vaccination [35]. • *E.g.*, cooking oil, LED television sets, smartphone, and rice. • IndiGo: offering 10% discount for air tickets [36] • Central Bank of India: 25bps higher return/interest rate [36].	• Autorickshaw's driver: impound the autorickshaw and impose a fine; • Shop & Commercial: sealed if the worker and owner do not receive any vaccination [37]. • Aurangabad: not allowed to enter historic sites and monuments [38].
Hong Kong	• Government officials get the vaccines first • Cathay Pacific and HK Express provide 50,000 air tickets as prizes of a lucky draw [39] • Jardine Matheson launches $10 million prizes for the lucky draw [40].	• Vaccine Pass: People (except those getting exemption) who are not vaccinated cannot enter restaurants, entertainment venues government buildings, *etc* [41].
Japan	• The Gunma Prefectural Government: holding a lottery with the vehicle and travel coupons as prizes [42]. • Giving subsidies to clinics and hospitals if they meet the target of vaccination (>100,000 yen per day) [43].	• N/A

(Table 3) cont.....

Country/City	Incentive	Penalty
South Korea	• Exemption from fines is given to overstayers if they complete the vaccination [44].	• There are a limited number of people who do not get a vaccination in a team activity, including weddings, outdoor sports, and restaurants [45].
Taiwan	• Taipei and Taichung: Give NT$200 voucher after vaccination • Offering NT$500 vouchers to the elderly if they get a vaccination.	• Full vaccination is needed if the citizens want to enter bars and nightclubs [46].
Singapore	• A $30 voucher would be given to the one who accompanies the elderly to vaccination [47]. • Offering mobile and home vaccination teams [47].	• Not allowing the unvaccinated employees to return to the workplace [48]. • The termination of employment because of rejecting vaccination is not considered an unreasonable dismissal [48].
China	• Beijing: One health center gives 5.5 pounds of eggs to 60 years and above residents [49]. • Shanghai: Take photos with celebrities; lottery; cash (200 yuan-1500 yuan); Disney Park tickets [50].	• Not allowed to enter schools, hospitals, and parks before taking vaccination in some county-level governments [51].

5. THE ADOPTION OF BLOCKCHAIN IN THE VACCINE SUPPLY CHAIN

Information technology is important to supply chain management (SCM). Three main factors increase the importance of timely and accurate information. First, offering efficient and effective services (including order status and delivery schedules) become mainstream in SCM. Second, making use of information can decrease the inventory and optimize human resources to meet the competitive level. Third, during strategic planning and deploying resources, information flow plays an important role [52]. If there is a lack of reliable information technology, it can cause some problems in the supply chain. In 2021, there were more than 8,000 expired vaccines disposed of in Canada [53]. In the United Kingdom, 170,000 doses of vaccines faced the risk of expiry [54]. In Lithuania and Poland, there were 20,000 and 73,000 doses of vaccines disposed of because of expiry, respectively [55]. The reports show that many developed countries were facing a problem of surplus vaccines. One of the reasons causing this situation is because of the government's lack of information about the demand for the vaccine and the supply chain.

In the blockchain, every block owns a variety number (*i.e.* 256 bits), which is produced with unity by an analytical algorithm. The blocks are associated with one another regarding the past block's number which produces an independent and secure chain. Before incorporating blocks into the blockchain, they require to be verified, which may potentially be with the appearance of evidence of work which is identified as 'blockchain mining'. Then, the block comes to be included in the network's immutable and auditable blockchain after confirmation. Also, there is an incorporated defense method. Specifically, every corruption that is discovered by the blockchain as vicious (about modified block changes in the hash situations of all the blocks) will be defended and captured. In the infected node, the corrupted block will be rectified accordingly [56]. Based on the structure of blockchain, it can make sure the supply chain is safe and transparent.

Blockchain belongs to decentralized technology, which owns some unique features including "impenetrable information infrastructure, transparency, and cryptographic encryption tools" [57]. It is time stamping, and real-time tracking [58]. Blockchain technology can help the organization to collect necessary data from the stakeholder. Then, based on the data, it can be analyzed and developed into big-scale data [59]. Because of decentralization, there is no intermediary in the supply chain. As a result, all the participants in the blockchain own the right to verify the record and whole database of the blockchain without any third-party help [60].

Information sharing is one of the important features of blockchain. Point-to-point transfer mode is the main information exchange way in the supply chain. Thus, because of a lack of sharing mechanisms, the security and transparency of trading information become uncertain. Besides, lacking information means the parties in the supply chain cannot get enough data to analyse demand in the market. It can lead to a serious bullwhip effect when the failing demand forecasting and blind production appear [61].

Based on the features of blockchain, it is used as a platform to analyze and track data and manage supply chain processes [62]. For example, in previous years, because of incomplete information, it caused many problems in the vaccine supply chain. For example, in 2016, there was research showing that the Nigerian government was facing the problem of over-storage of the vaccine while they did not own enough storage facilities [63]. This waste is because the government does not have enough data about the demand. After implementing blockchain into health logistics, it can enhance the efficiency and transparency of the distribution processes so that the parties can track the vaccine and make better management in the storage environment and condition of delivery [64]. In India, there is a problem of fake COVID-19 vaccination. More than 2,000 citizens get a fake vaccination [65]. Blockchain technology can avoid the problem of fake vaccines by using QR codes and digital signatures so that the government can check the information about the vaccine through the QR code to confirm whether it is fake

[66]. Besides, based on real-time information, it can reduce miscommunication issues [67]. Furthermore, based on real-time information, the accuracy of forecasting can be increased. Therefore, the problem of over-storage can be reduced.

In the healthcare supply chain (HCSC), blockchain technology focuses on "supply chain management, patient data management, clinical trials and data security, drug traceability" *etc* [68]. Besides, as mentioned above, the medical company can enroll their medical on the database of blockchain. In doing so, all the parties in the blockchain can find information about the drugs (*e.g.* the production time, place of the production, and producer) through timestamps [40]. Thus, the possibility of misusing fake drugs can be minimized.

6. EMERGENCY LOGISTICS & VACCINE LOGISTICS IN COVID-19

Under COVID-19, the demand for medicine and medical resources, including N95 face masks, medical oxygen, and protective equipment (PPE) has increased. In response, emergency logistics and vaccine logistics become more important than before.

Before the disaster and in the end, the actions of emergency logistics are not stopped [69]. Emergency logistics aims to avoid the interruption in supply and can get the response and running immediately [70]. There are three main components in emergency logistics: inventory management, transportation management, and information system [71].

For inventory management, the planning of the distribution routing model is built up by the forecast of the demand and the estimated period [72]. In the beginning, there are half of the face masks that are produced in China [18]. When the export of face masks is decreased because of shortage, in other countries it is hard to get enough face masks to satisfy the demand of nationals. Hence, there is not enough inventory to support the running of emergency logistics at the beginning of COVID-19.

For transportation management, emergency logistics focus on shortening transportation time. As such, it needs to build up a distribution routing model so that it can minimize the delivery delay and total travel time [73]. However, under COVID-19, because of the impact of the lockdown, the procurement of raw materials and the shipping of goods are also affected [74]. Thus, even though emergency logistics has a model to deal with unexpected situations, because of the different countries' regulations, the efficiency of the logistics is affected.

For the information system, building up a reliable communication network can help the logistics system to get a "fast, real-time and accurate flow of the information" which is useful to predict and control the disaster and the distribution of emergency goods [75]. However, in COVID-19, the communication network was interrupted because of a limited information system. According to research, in Sub-Saharan Africa (SSA), there are more than 500 million people who cannot use the Internet [76]. Thus, it is hard for the nationals to get the newest information about COVID-19 and they cannot report when they suffer from the pandemic. It made it hard for the government of SSA to collect information about patients so the accuracy of the forecast for the demand for vaccines and medical resources decreased.

Since vaccines can control the pandemic significantly, the importance of vaccine logistics has increased. The cold chain is one of the important components of vaccine logistics. Cold chain logistics means that during production, storage, transportation, sales, and final consumption, the products are under prescriptive temperatures which are set by the characteristics of the goods so that the quality of the goods can be ensured [77].

Under the cold chain, products will be shipped by refrigerated cargo ships, refrigerated railcars, refrigerated containers, and refrigerated trucks [78]. Cold chain equipment (CCEs) is one of the components of the cold chain. They include "cold room/walk-in coolers and freezer room/walk-in freezers" [34]. The quality of vaccines can be affected by heat, light, and changes in the environment [79]. According to research, most vaccines should be stored at +2°C to +8°C so the potency and protective effect of the vaccine will not be affected [80].

There are three distinct temperature bands of the refrigerators: medium-temperature refrigeration (2°C to 8°C), low-temperature refrigeration (–50°C to –15°C), and ultra-low-temperature (ULT) refrigeration (–80°C to –60°C) [81]. However, the inventory of developing ULT refrigerators is quite high so the selling price of the refrigerator would not be low [82]. The initial capital cost is around $12,000-$40,000 USD. Compared to the typical vaccine refrigerator ($3,499 USD), it needs more than $8000 USD (TempArmour, n.d.). Besides, the maintenance costs are also high so it is hard for developing countries to own enough ULT refrigerators to store the special needed vaccine. However, there are two main problems in vaccine logistics faced by most governments.

First, the optimal cold chain temperature for the vaccine used for COVID-19 is different from the validated vaccine. Until January 2022, there are ten vaccines approved by the World Health Organization (WHO) [20]. However, six kinds of vaccines were approved before May 2021. They are Pfizer/BioNTech, AstraZeneca, Covishield, Janssen, Moderna, and Sinopharm.

According to Table **4**, there were three main types of vaccines whose storage temperatures were not in the range of major optimal cold chain temperatures. That means the existing transportation, equipment, and warehouse may not have the ability to keep the vaccines. Take India as an example, India owns around 28,000 cold chain units. However, all the units cannot transport vaccines below −25 °C [83]. For developing countries, it is hard to procure a great number of ULT freezers in a short period. Lack of suitable freezers causes difficulties in transporting the vaccine which has special temperature requirements.

Table 4. Storage temperatures of vaccines.

Vaccine	Storage Temperature
Pfizer/BioNTech	-60°C to -86°C
AstraZeneca	2°C to 8°C
Covishield	2°C to 8°C
Janssen	-20°C
Moderna	-25°C to -15°C
Sinopharm	2°C to 8°C

Source: WHO [84]; AstraZeneca [85]

Secondly, not all countries own enough cold chain facilities to store and transport the vaccine. According to the World Bank [86], there are around 50% of countries that own enough capacities for the cold chain which are used for the normal kinds of vaccines, not included for ULT storage. That means there are near half of the countries that do not have the capacity to store vaccines, even though the required temperature is just 2°C to 8°C. For these kinds of countries, vaccine logistics would be affected.

CONCLUSION

In this chapter, we mainly provide the general situation of an influenza pandemic in the world and Hong Kong. To mitigate the impact of the COVID-19 pandemic and stop the transmission of the virus, the development of vaccines seems a 'sole' solution in the time of the COVID-19 pandemic. As expected, the use of blockchain in the vaccine supply chain may further reinforce the safety and efficiency of healthcare supply chain management in the future.

REFERENCES

[1] Fineberg HV. Pandemic preparedness and response :Lessons from the H1N1 influenza of 2009. N Engl J Med 2014; 370(14): 1335-42.
[http://dx.doi.org/10.1056/NEJMra1208802] [PMID: 24693893]

[2] Peckham R. Viral surveillance and the 1968 Hong Kong flu pandemic. J Glob Hist 2020; 15(3): 444-58.
[http://dx.doi.org/10.1017/S1740022820000224]

[3] Hung LS. The SARS epidemic in Hong Kong: What lessons have we learned? J R Soc Med 2003; 96(8): 374-8.
[http://dx.doi.org/10.1177/014107680309600803] [PMID: 12893851]

[4] Ebola virus disease. WHO | World Health Organization. Available from: https://www.who.int/news-room/fact-sheets/detail/ebola-virus-disease (2021, February 23).

[5] About HIV. Centers for Disease Control and Prevention. Available from: https://www.cdc.gov/hiv/basics/whatishiv.html (2021, June 1).

[6] CDC. 1968 Pandemic (H3N2 virus). Available from: https://www.cdc.gov/flu/pandemic-resources/1968-pandemic.html (2019, January 22).

[7] Cholera. WHO | World Health Organization. Available from: https://www.who.int/news-room/fac--sheets/detail/cholera (2021, February 5).

[8] Department of Health. Ebola virus disease. Centre for Health Protection. Available from: https://www.chp.gov.hk/en/healthtopics/content/24/34397.html (2020, April 24).

[9] Monkeypox. Centre for Health Protection. Available from: https://www.chp.gov.hk/en/healthtopics/content/24/101721.html (2022, May 24).

[10] Plague. Centers for Disease Control and Prevention. Available from: https://www.cdc.gov/plague/index.html (2020, July 23).

[11] Severe acute respiratory syndrome (SARS). WHO | World Health. Available from: https://www.who.int/health-topics/severe-acute-respiratory-syndrome#tab=tab_3 (2019, November 1).

[12] Smallpox. WHO | World Health Organization. Available from: https://www.who.int/health-topics/smallpox (2019, November 1).

[13] Liu YC, Kuo RL, Shih SR. COVID-19: The first documented coronavirus pandemic in history. Biomed J 2020; 43(4): 328-33.
[http://dx.doi.org/10.1016/j.bj.2020.04.007] [PMID: 32387617]

[14] Tanu S. Review for Coronavirus disease 2019 (COVID-19) vaccines: A concise review. Nat Pub Heal Emerg Collec 2020; 87(4): 281-6.

[15] Hu B, Guo H, Zhou P, Shi ZL. Characteristics of SARS-CoV-2 and COVID-19. Nat Rev Microbiol 2021; 19(3): 141-54.
[http://dx.doi.org/10.1038/s41579-020-00459-7] [PMID: 33024307]

[16] World Health Organization. Coronavirus disease (COVID-19): Vaccines. 2022. Available from: https://www.who.int/news-room/questions-and-answers/item/coronavirus-disease-(cov-d-19-
-
vaccines?gclid=CjwKCAjw14uVBhBEEiwAaufYx5lY0XAW2kAZLIERJ5l5yA2Py0VbTUTdsvN-9Y HY83b7dTOIHVpchoCltcQAvD_BwE&topicsurvey=v8kj13

[17] Keni R, Alexander A, Nayak PG, Mudgal J, Nandakumar K. COVID-19: Emergence, spread, possible treatments, and global burden. Front Public Health 2020; 8: 216.
[http://dx.doi.org/10.3389/fpubh.2020.00216] [PMID: 32574299]

[18] Sharma A, Ahmad Farouk I, Lal SK. COVID-19: A review on the novel coronavirus disease

evolution, transmission, detection, control and prevention. Viruses 2021; 13(2): 202.
[http://dx.doi.org/10.3390/v13020202] [PMID: 33572857]

[19]   UNICEF. Japan donates over US$11 million to UNICEF to keep COVID-19 vaccines cool in Latin America and the Caribbean. Available from: https://www.unicef.org/lac/en/press-releases/japa--donates-over-11-million-dollars-to-unicef-to-keep-covid-19-vaccines-cool (2021, August 12).

[20]   WHO. COVID-19 Situation in WHO South-East Asia Region. 2022. Available from: https://experience.arcgis.com/experience/56d2642cb379485ebf78371e744b8c6a

[21]   Wan KM, Ka-ki Ho L, Wong NWM, Chiu A. Fighting COVID-19 in Hong Kong: The effects of community and social mobilization. World Dev 2020; 134: 105055.
[http://dx.doi.org/10.1016/j.worlddev.2020.105055] [PMID: 32834373]

[22]   Zhu G, Chou MC, Tsai CW. Lessons learned from the COVID-19 pandemic exposing the shortcomings of current supply chain operations: A long-term prescriptive offering. Sustainability 2020; 12(14): 5858.
[http://dx.doi.org/10.3390/su12145858]

[23]   Alam ST, Ahmed S, Ali SM, Sarker S, Kabir G, ul-Islam A. Challenges to COVID-19 vaccine supply chain: Implications for sustainable development goals. Int J Prod Econ 2021; 239: 108193.
[http://dx.doi.org/10.1016/j.ijpe.2021.108193] [PMID: 34121813]

[24]   Kim SS, Wong AKF, Han H, Yeung MWV. How does the COVID-19 pandemic influence travel industry employees in Hong Kong? Structural relationships among airline crew's job-related stressors, mental health and other consequences. Asia Pac J Tour Res 2022; 27(1): 69-85.
[http://dx.doi.org/10.1080/10941665.2021.1998161]

[25]   Ye H, Law R. Impact of COVID-19 on hospitality and tourism education: A case study of Hong Kong. J Teach Travel Tour 2021; 21(4): 428-36.
[http://dx.doi.org/10.1080/15313220.2021.1875967]

[26]   Jones P, Comfort D. The COVID-19 crisis and sustainability in the hospitality industry. Int J Contemp Hosp Manag 2020; 32(10): 3037-50.
[http://dx.doi.org/10.1108/IJCHM-04-2020-0357]

[27]   Tessema GA, Kinfu Y, Dachew BA, *et al.* The COVID-19 pandemic and healthcare systems in Africa: A scoping review of preparedness, impact and response. BMJ Glob Health 2021; 6(12): e007179.
[http://dx.doi.org/10.1136/bmjgh-2021-007179] [PMID: 34853031]

[28]   Lam HY, Lau CCA, Wong CH, *et al.* A review of epidemiology and public health control measures of COVID-19 variants in Hong Kong, December 2020 to June 2021. IJID Regions 2022; 2: 16-24.
[http://dx.doi.org/10.1016/j.ijregi.2021.11.002] [PMID: 35721421]

[29]   Caddy S. Developing a vaccine for covid-19. BMJ 2020; 369: m1790.
[http://dx.doi.org/10.1136/bmj.m1790]

[30]   Saleh A, Qamar S, Tekin A, Singh R, Kashyap R. Vaccine development throughout history. Cureus 2021; 13(7): e16635.
[http://dx.doi.org/10.7759/cureus.16635] [PMID: 34462676]

[31]   Sharma O, Sultan AA, Ding H, Triggle CR. A review of the progress and challenges of developing a vaccine for COVID-19. Front Immunol 2020; 11: 585354.
[http://dx.doi.org/10.3389/fimmu.2020.585354] [PMID: 33163000]

[32]   Kaur SP, Gupta V. COVID-19 Vaccine: A comprehensive status report. Virus Res 2020; 288: 198114.
[http://dx.doi.org/10.1016/j.virusres.2020.198114] [PMID: 32800805]

[33]   Mohamed NA, Solehan HM, Mohd Rani MD, Ithnin M, Che Isahak CI. Knowledge, acceptance and perception on COVID-19 vaccine among Malaysians: A web-based survey. PLoS One 2021; 16(8): e0256110.
[http://dx.doi.org/10.1371/journal.pone.0256110] [PMID: 34388202]

[34]   Kumar G, Gupta S. Assessment of cold chain equipments and their management in government health facilities in a District of Delhi: A cross-sectional descriptive study. Indian J Public Health 2020; 64(1): 22-6.
[http://dx.doi.org/10.4103/ijph.IJPH_457_18] [PMID: 32189678]

[35]   Sarkar AR. Indian states offer TVs, fridges and smartphones as vaccine drive lags. 2021. Available from: https://www.independent.co.uk/asia/india/india-maharashtra-covid-vaccine-incent-ves-b1968440.html

[36]   IndiGo n.d.. Vaxi Fare for our vaccinated fliers. Available from: https://www.goindigo.in/add-o--services/vaxi-fare-for-vaccinated-fliers.html

[37]   Agarwal R. Incentives India Inc. is offering to Covid 19 vaccinated Individuals. 2021. Available from: https://www.goodreturns.in/personal-finance/planning/incentives-india-inc-is-offering-to--ovid-19-vaccinated-individuals-1213604.html

[38]   New Delhi Television. In Maharashtra District, This Is Penalty For Not Taking 1st Vaccine Shot. 2021. Available from: https://www.ndtv.com/india-news/coronavirus-in-maharashtras-aurang-bad-district-this-is-penalty-for-not-taking-1st-vaccine-shot-2621358

[39]   Sassy Hong Kong. 2021.The Best Hong Kong COVID Vaccine Lucky Draws & Discounts You Need To Know About. Available from: https://www.sassyhongkong.com/hk-covid-vaccine-discounts-l-cky-draws-whats-on/

[40]   Anusha R, Prasad S. Blockchain technology for supply chain, health care, intellectual property rights, e-voting. TurkJ Comp MathemEduc 2021; 12(10): 1873-8.

[41]   HKSARG. COVID-19 thematic website, together, we fight the virus, home. 2022. Available from: https://www.coronavirus.gov.hk/eng/index.html#What_is_COVID-19

[42]   Nakai S, Hanafusa N, Masakane I, *et al.* An overview of regular dialysis treatment in Japan (as of 31 December 2012). Ther Apher Dial 2014; 18(6): 535-602.
[http://dx.doi.org/10.1111/1744-9987.12281] [PMID: 25523509]

[43]   Kyodo News. Japan readies higher incentives for clinics to give COVID-19 shots. 2021. Available from: https://english.kyodonews.net/news/2021/05/f012ccd20dce-japan-readies-higher-incentive--for-clinics-to-give-covid-19-shots.html

[44]   Yonhap News Agency. Seoul announces incentives for vaccinated overstayers. 2021. Available from: https://en.yna.co.kr/view/AEN20211008005200315

[45]   Seo JE. Vaccine perks added as social distancing extended two weeks. 2021. Available from: https://koreajoongangdaily.joins.com/2021/10/01/national/socialAffairs/covid19-socia--distancing-vaccine-incentives/20211001164428881.html

[46]   Wang A. Taiwan to mandate COVID-19 vaccination proof for entertainment venues. 2022. Available from: https://www.channelnewsasia.com/asia/taiwan-mandate-covid-19-vaccination--roof-entertainment-venues-2447616

[47]   Ministry   of   Health.   VACCINATION   INCENTIVE.   2021.   Available   from: https://www.moh.gov.sg/news-highlights/details/vaccination-incentive/

[48]   Ministry of Manpower. Updated advisory on COVID-19 vaccination at the workplace. 2022. Available   from: https://www.mom.gov.sg/covid-19/advisory-on-covid-19-vaccination-in-emp-oyment-settings

[49]   Jacob C. Asian countries try a new strategy to get people on board with vaccines: Free prizes. 2021. Available   from: https://www.cnbc.com/2021/08/10/vaccine-incentives-asia-countries-give-awa--land-gold-cattle-homes.html

[50]   James G. From cash to celebrity photos and even temporary boyfriends: What Shanghai is offering for COVID-19   vaccinations.   2021.   Available   from: https://supchina.com/2021/06/29/from-cash--o-celebrity-photos-and-even-temporary-boyfriends-what-shanghai-is-offering-

for-covid-19-vaccinations/

[51] Westcott B. Unvaccinated people in parts of China to be denied access to hospitals, parks and schools. 2021. Available from: https://edition.cnn.com/2021/07/15/china/vaccine-china-restrictions-zhejing-jiangxi-intl-hnk/index.html

[52] Moharana HS, Murty JS, Senapati SK, Khuntia K. Importance of information technology for effective supply chain management. Int J Mod Eng Res 2011; 1(2): 747-51.

[53] Aziz S. COVID-19 vaccine wastage concerns in Canada as Moderna doses expire this week. 2021. Available from: https://globalnews.ca/news/8079728/moderna-covid-vaccine-expired-doses-canada

[54] Elgot J. NHS urged to redistribute near-expiry vaccines as take-up slows in young. 2021. Available from: https://www.theguardian.com/society/2021/aug/01/nhs-urged-to-redistribute-near-expiry-coronavirus-vaccines-as-take-up-slows-in-young

[55] Damiani A. NHS urged to redistribute near-expiry vaccines as take-up slows in young. 2021. Available from: https://www.euractiv.com/section/coronavirus/news/eu-countries-are-throwing--way-expired-vaccine-doses/

[56] Dutta P, Choi T M, Somani S, Butala R. Blockchain technology in supply chain operations: Applications, challenges and research opportunities. Transp Res E Logist Transp Rev 2020; 142: 102067.

[57] Marbouh D, Abbasi T, Maasmi F, *et al.* Blockchain for COVID-19: Review, opportunities, and a trusted tracking system. Arab J Sci Eng 2020; 45(12): 9895-911.
[http://dx.doi.org/10.1007/s13369-020-04950-4] [PMID: 33072472]

[58] Torky M, Hassanien AE. COVID-19 Blockchain Framework: Innovative Approach. 2020. Available from: https://arxiv.org/ftp/arxiv/papers/2004/2004.06081.pdf

[59] Sharma A, Bahl S, Bagha AK, Javaid M, Shukla DK, Haleem A. Blockchain technology and its applications to combat COVID-19 pandemic. Res Biomed Eng 2020; 1-8.

[60] Azizi N, Malekzadeh H, Akhavan P, Haass O, Saremi S, Mirjalili S. IoT–blockchain: Harnessing the power of internet of thing and blockchain for smart supply chain. Sensors 2021; 21(18): 6048.
[http://dx.doi.org/10.3390/s21186048] [PMID: 34577261]

[61] Xue X, Dou J, Shang Y. Blockchain-driven supply chain decentralized operations–information sharing perspective. Bus Process Manag J 2020.

[62] Khubrani MM, Alam S. A detailed review of blockchain-based applications for protection against pandemic like COVID-19. TELKOMNIKA Telecommun Comp Electr Cont 2021; 19(4): 1185-96.
[http://dx.doi.org/10.12928/telkomnika.v19i4.18465]

[63] Shittu E, Harnly M, Whitaker S, Miller R. Reorganizing Nigeria's vaccine supply chain reduces need for additional storage facilities, but more storage is required. Health Aff 2016; 35(2): 293-300.
[http://dx.doi.org/10.1377/hlthaff.2015.1328] [PMID: 26858383]

[64] Antal C, Cioara T, Antal M, Anghel I. Blockchain platform for COVID-19 vaccine supply management. IEEE Open J Comput Soc 2021; 2: 164-78.
[http://dx.doi.org/10.1109/OJCS.2021.3067450]

[65] Mukherjee D, Maskey U, Ishak A, Sarfraz Z, Sarfraz A, Jaiswal V. Fake COVID-19 vaccination in India: An emerging dilemma? Postgrad Med J 2022; 98(e2): e115-6.
[http://dx.doi.org/10.1136/postgradmedj-2021-141003] [PMID: 37066530]

[66] Abid A, Cheikhrouhou S, Kallel S, Jmaiel M. NovidChain: Blockchain-based privacy-preserving platform for COVID-19 test/vaccine certificates. Softw Pract Exper 2022; 52(4): 841-67.
[http://dx.doi.org/10.1002/spe.2983] [PMID: 34226768]

[67] Kamenivskyy Y, Palisetti A, Hamze L, Saberi S. A blockchain-based solution for COVID-19 vaccine distribution. IEEE Eng Manage Rev 2022; 50(1): 43-53.
[http://dx.doi.org/10.1109/EMR.2022.3145656]

[68]   Reda M, Kanga DB, Fatima T, Azouazi M. Blockchain in health supply chain management: State of art challenges and opportunities. Procedia Comput Sci 2020; 175: 706-9.
[http://dx.doi.org/10.1016/j.procs.2020.07.104]

[69]   Shen L, Tao F, Shi Y, Qin R. Optimization of location-routing problem in emergency logistics considering carbon emissions. Int J Environ Res Public Health 2019; 16(16): 2982.
[http://dx.doi.org/10.3390/ijerph16162982] [PMID: 31430997]

[70]   Banomyong R, Sopadang A. Using Monte Carlo simulation to refine emergency logistics response models: A case study. Int J Phys Distrib Logist Manag 2010; 40(8/9): 709-21.
[http://dx.doi.org/10.1108/09600031011079346]

[71]   Lau Y, Jiamian Z, Ng Adolf KY, Panahi R. Implications of a pandemic outbreak risk: A discussion on china's emergency logistics in the era of coronavirus disease 2019 (COVID-19). J Int Logist Trade 2020; 18(3): 127-35.
[http://dx.doi.org/10.24006/jilt.2020.18.3.127]

[72]   Özdamar L, Ekinci E, Küçükyazici B. Emergency logistics planning in natural disasters. Ann Oper Res 2004; 129(1-4): 217-45.
[http://dx.doi.org/10.1023/B:ANOR.0000030690.27939.39]

[73]   Huang X, Song L. An emergency logistics distribution routing model for unexpected events. Ann Oper Res 2018; 269(1-2): 223-39.
[http://dx.doi.org/10.1007/s10479-016-2300-7]

[74]   Balfour H. COVID-19 update: coronavirus and the pharmaceutical supply chain. 2020. Available from: https://www.europeanpharmaceuticalreview.com/article/116145/covid-19-update-coronavi-us-and-the-pharmaceutical-supply-chain/

[75]   Fu L. Research on the construction of the emergency logistics system in the large state-owned enterprises. Open J Soc Sci 2014; 2(9): 59-63.
[http://dx.doi.org/10.4236/jss.2014.29010]

[76]   Ogbo E, Brown T, Gant J, Davis A, Sicker D. The impact of over-the-top services on preferences for mobile services: A conjoint analysis of users in nigeria. J Inform Pol 2021; 11(1): 403-43.
[http://dx.doi.org/10.5325/jinfopoli.11.2021.0403]

[77]   Kuang M, Du Y, Kuang D, Zhu X. Research on the optimization of urban cold chain logistics system based on the example of guangzhou. J Phys Conf Ser 2021; 1746(1): 012074.
[http://dx.doi.org/10.1088/1742-6596/1746/1/012074]

[78]   Heap RD. Cold chain performance issues now and in the future. Bulletin of the IIR 2006; 4: 1-13.

[79]   Dumpa N, Goel K, Guo Y, *et al.* Stability of vaccines. AAPS PharmSciTech 2019; 20(2): 42.
[http://dx.doi.org/10.1208/s12249-018-1254-2] [PMID: 30610415]

[80]   Centre for Health Protection. Chapter 6 - Requirements on Vaccine Storage and Handling under VSS. 2021.   Available   from:
https://www.chp.gov.hk/files/pdf/vssdg_ch6_vaccine_storage_and_handling.pdf

[81]   Hwang Y, Greenfield B, Kranz B, *et al.* Transporting and storing COVID-19 vaccines. ASHRAE J 2022; 64(2).

[82]   Fortune. (2020). Ultra-low Temperature Freezer Market Size, Share & Report [2027]. Available from: https://www.fortunebusinessinsights.com/ultra-low-temperature-freezer-market-104479

[83]   Colehower. The challenges to vaccine distribution affecting everyone. 2021. Available from: https://healthcare-digital.com/procurement-and-supply-chain/challenges-vaccine-distri-ution-affecting-everyone

[84]   World Health Organization. Job aid: How to manage storage and distribution of COVID-19 Vaccine Janssen delivered at -20°C and +2 to +8°C temperatures?. 2021. Available from: https://www.who.int/publications/m/item/job-aid-covid-19-vaccine-janssen

[85] AstraZeneca. Serum Institute of India obtains emergency use authorisation in India for AstraZeneca's COVID-19 vaccine. 2021. Available from: https://www.astrazeneca.com/media-centre/pres--releases/2021/serum-institute-of-india-obtains-emergency-use-authorisation-i--india-for-astrazenecas-covid-19-vaccine.html

[86] World Bank. Assessing country readiness for COVID-19 vaccines. 2021. Available from: https://documents1.worldbank.org/curated/en/467291615997445437/pdf/Assessing-Country-Readiness-for-COVID-19-Vaccines-First-Insights-from-the-Assessment-Rollout.pdf

CHAPTER 5

Anti-epidemic Measures of a Community

Abstract: In this chapter, the authors mainly highlight the key anti-epidemic measures adopted by a community. A total of 14 illustrative examples are discussed to demonstrate the different measures adopted in response to the COVID-19 pandemic. Details of the measures are provided, including photos, such as in a gym, hospitals, swimming pools, catering premises, a cinema, theme parks (*i.e.* Ocean Park and Disneyland), the Hong Kong Airport, schools, public markets, an elderly home, a church, museums, the Hong Kong Coliseum and public transportation. The anti-epidemic measures were effective in controlling the spread of COVID-19 during the different waves in the past 3 years. The anti-epidemic measures may provide valuable insights into the practices and preparation of other countries for the post-COVID-19-pandemic future.

Keywords: Anti-epidemic measures, Community.

1. INRODUCTION

During the COVID-19 pandemic, numerous public facilities and venues implement stringent anti-epidemic measures so as to minimize the transmission of the virus in the community. In this chapter, we have highlighted the common areas including gym room, hospital, swimming pool, catering premises, cinema, theme park (*i.e.*, Ocean Park and Disneyland), Hong Kong airport, school, public market, elderly home, church, museum, Hong Kong Coliseum, and public transportation to demonstrate the different anti-epidemic measures via the photos and key regulations. The details are provided in different sections.

2. GYM

2.1. For Users

1. Must bring their own equipment, such as yoga mats and/or boxing gloves.

2. Must maintain a social distance from others at all times whilst in the fitness centre; must not remove their face mask.

3. Must maintain a distance of at least 1.5 m from others, such as when taking a shower or eating in the designated places.

4. Must check their temperature before visiting; in case of a fever or respiratory tract infection symptoms or sudden loss of taste/smell, they must cancel their visit and seek medical assistance when feeling ill.

5. Must mask up and seek medical assistance as soon as possible when feeling ill.

6. Must properly clean and disinfect lockers before and after use.

2.2. Physical Setting

1. Set up a temperature monitoring station with a heat detector at the entrance; employees took visitors' temperature at the entrance and refused entry to those with a fever.

2. Provided adequate hand-cleaning facilities at the entrance, fitness stations, near the equipment, and around the facility, such as hand rubbing liquid containing 70%–80% alcohol.

3. Provided surgical masks to users in need.

4. Properly cleaned and disinfected equipment before use.

5. Installed additional air fresheners.

6. Required users to follow the face mask regulations; asked a registered specialist contractor to assess and report the air change rate six times or more per hour or install air purification equipment based on the specifications provided by the Food and Environmental Hygiene Department (FEHD); listed the air purification equipment brand and model.

7. Added water dispensers in the facility.

During the COVID-19 pandemic in 2019, to prevent cross-infection (from a water bottle or nozzle accidentally touching the nozzle of the water dispenser and its protective device), the gym prohibited users from using the jet water dispenser and encouraged them to bring their own container (*e.g.* cup or water bottle) to hold the water from the water dispenser. Gym users were also advised to refrain from washing their hands or cleaning their personal belongings with the water dispenser. The water dispensers were properly cleaned and maintained regularly. The key COVID-19 information related to the gym room can be accessed [1] and the relevant photos are provided in Figs. (**1** - **4**).

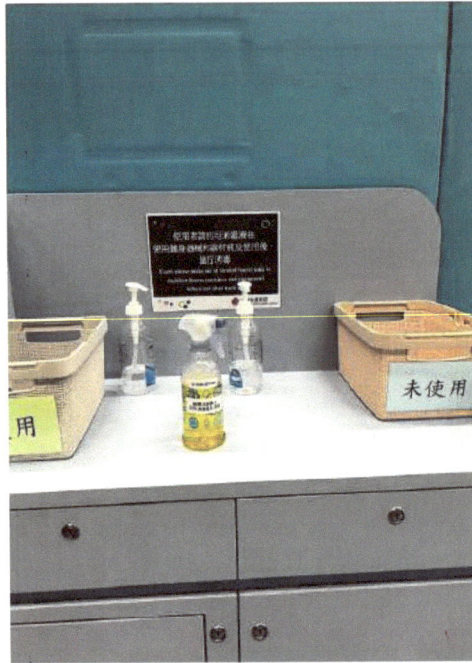

Source: Authors

Fig. (1). Gym room during the covid-19 pandemic.

Source: Authors

Fig. (2). Gym room during the covid-19 pandemic.

Source: Authors

Fig. (3). Gym room during the covid-19 pandemic.

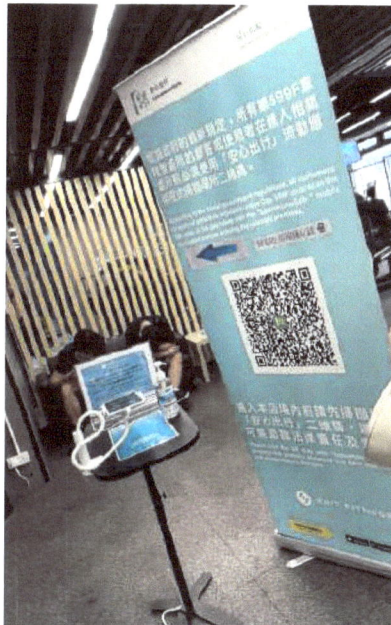

Source: Authors

Fig. (4). Gym room during the covid-19 pandemic.

3. HOSPITALS

In response to the outbreak of COVID-19 in Hong Kong in 2019, the Hospital Authority converted one or two general wards in each cluster into standard negative pressure wards, provided around 500 additional standard negative pressure beds as 'second isolation wards' and increased the number of second-line isolation beds to around 660 by the end of August 2020. The following key COVID-19 information associated with hospitals can be found in [2] and the relevant photos are given in Figs. (**5** and **6**).

Fig. (5). Hospital during the covid-19 pandemic.

Fig. (6). Hospital during the covid-19 pandemic.

1. Visitors must scan the 'Safe Travel' QR code when entering public hospitals. People over the age of 65 years, those with a disability and difficulty using the 'Safe Travel' application and those who are exempted from complying with the requirements must complete a specific form to register.

2. Hospital personnel must wear surgical masks at all times.

3. The temperature of visitors and personnel must be checked before entering the hospital.

4. Visitors must declare their health condition for risk assessment before entering the hospital.

5. Visitors and personnel must wash their hands thoroughly before entering and leaving the hospital.

6. Visitors must provide a negative result of a COVID-19 nucleic acid test taken within the last 48 hours or a negative result of a COVID-19 rapid antigen test taken within the last 24 hours before visiting a hospital.

7. Additional facilities were installed in hospitals.

A. Two exhaust fans were installed in every six-person bedroom in the ward.

B. High-efficiency particulate-absorbing filter exhaust devices were installed on windows.

C. Additional doors were added to the entrance of wards to create a buffer room to stabilise the negative air pressure in the wards.

3.1. Hong Kong Sanatorium & Hospital

Hospital personnel who suspect or confirm a patient to be infected by a virus that can be transmitted through the air/droplets will arrange for the patient to stay in the ward with pandemic prevention facilities, according to the situation, to prevent the virus from spreading to the other parts of the hospital. Hospital personnel will transfer the other patients to appropriate wards according to their condition and the severity of their illness to reduce their chances of cross-infection in the hospital.

3.2. Special Facilities

• Negative air pressure pumping system - Airflow is controlled through negative air pressure to ensure that the outdoor air pressure is higher than the air pressure in the front room, and the air pressure in the front room is higher than that in the ward, where the air pressure in the toilet is the lowest. This arrangement can ensure that air will flow only out of a room into the ward and discharged through the toilet, so air containing pathogens cannot flow back into the room, thereby reducing the risk of infection in the hospital.

- Ultraviolet light exhaust port - The exhaust port is equipped with purple light, which can directly disinfect and kill pathogens released by patients when coughing or sneezing.
- Double-door design – Double doors were installed in front rooms located outside airborne isolation wards, with one door at the front and one door at the back of the room. The two doors cannot be opened at the same time to prevent bacteria and viruses from flowing out of the room through the air. The door switch has an inductive design, and medical personnel need only to wave their hands in front of the door latch without touching it to automatically open the door, thereby reducing the risk of infection.

4. SWIMMING POOLS

1. All swimming pool staff must comply with the vaccination requirements, specifically, they must have at least two doses of the COVID-19 vaccine.

2. All swimming pool users must comply with the vaccination requirements of the 'Vaccination Pass', unless exempted.

3. Individuals in the swimming pools must wear a mask all the time, except when (a) swimming; (b) drinking water, when necessary; (c) taking a shower; (d) walking from the locker room to a swimming pool; (e) walking to a different swimming pool; and (f) when doing warm-up exercises with a distance of at least 1.5 m from any other person or with some form of partition. Coaches must wear a mask all the time when instructing trainees.

4. The number of visitors must not exceed 50% of the original capacity to enable swimmers to maintain a safe distance from other swimmers.

5. The water in all public swimming pools is continuously filtered and disinfected during operating hours, and the Leisure and Cultural Services Department (LCSD) closely monitors the water quality in pools and regularly collects water samples for testing.

The aforementioned swimming pool COVID-19 information can be accessible to [3].

5. CATERING PREMISES

5.1. For Customers

1. Must comply with the COVID-19 vaccination requirements of the 'Vaccination Pass'.

2. Only up to eight people are allowed per ladle.

3. Dining after midnight is prohibited.

4. Live performances and dancing activities are prohibited.

5. Must comply with the COVID-19 vaccination requirements of the 'Vaccination Pass', except for those under the age of 12 years and those with an exemption certificate with a QR code issued by a doctor.

6. Must present their vaccination record or an exemption certificate or a QR code for their rehabilitation record for scanning before entering.

7. Must accomplish a specific form if they do not have a QR code for their vaccination record, except those under the age of 12 years who are accompanied by an adult.

8. Banquets are limited to 120 people.

9. Must use the 'Travel with Peace of Mind' mobile application.

5.2. For Employees

1. All employees involved in operations must comply with the COVID-19 vaccination requirements of the 'Vaccination Pass'.

2. Employees unfit for vaccination owing to health reasons with a COVID-19 Medical Vaccination Exemption Certificate must complete the specified form to report to the employer and get tested for the virus every 7 days.

3. All employees (including those who have recovered from the virus or have a vaccination medical exemption certificate) must take a rapid antigen test every 3 days before entering the premises.

5.3. For the Employer

1. Must ensure that the dining environment is well-ventilated, people who are not sitting at the same table are maintaining a distance of more than 1.5 m from one another and boxes, screens and/or partitions are separate.

The aforementioned catering premises COVID-19 information can be accessible to [4] and the relevant photos are shown in Figs. (**7** and **8**).

Fig. (7). Catering premises during the covid-19 pandemic.

Fig. (8). Catering premises during the covid-19 pandemic.

6. CINEMA

1. Capacity is limited to 50%, and no more than four seats in a row can be occupied continuously.

2. Face masks must be worn all the time, except when eating and/or drinking.

3. Visitors must take their temperature before entering.

4. Visitors must scan their 'Safe Travel' QR code before entering.

5. Visitors must show their 'Vaccination Pass' before entering.

6. Visitors must comply with the following rules when eating and/or drinking in the relatively closed screening hall:

a. All employees involved in the operation of the cinema must have received three doses of the COVID-19 vaccine or are recovered patients who have received two doses of the vaccine or have a medical exemption certificate.
b. All viewers attending the same screening in different theatres must have received three doses of the COVID-19 vaccine (children under the age of 12 years, and those who have recovered from the disease in the past 3 months and have received two doses of the vaccine were regarded as complying with the admission requirements).

The aforementioned cinema COVID-19 information can be accessible to [5].

7. THEME PARKS

7.1. Disneyland

- Temperature checks are conducted at all entrances to the resort, and all guests and entertainers must undergo temperature checks before entering the resort.
- Disinfectant hand-sanitising machines were installed in various locations in the resort, including the entrances and exits of amusement facilities, shops and restaurants.
- In addition to the basic pandemic prevention measures, crowd control measures were implemented, and social distancing stickers and signs were installed in queuing areas and performance viewing areas to remind guests to maintain an appropriate social distance from one another.
- Special seating arrangements were introduced in all the restaurants, food is covered or wrapped when served, cutlery is prepackaged and guests are encouraged to use contactless payment methods during checkout.

- Some interactive experiences, including cruises, close interactions and group photos with Disney friends, were suspended or adjusted.

7.2. Ocean Park

- All visitors and staff must have their body temperature checked before entering the park.
- All visitors and staff must wear a mask in all areas of the park (except when eating and/or drinking).
- The capacity of the park, as a whole, and of the individual amusement rides was reduced to half.
- All the theatres in the park adopted an interlaced seating arrangement.
- The 'Reservation Pass' mobile application increased the number of free reservations to a maximum of six attractions.
- Free hand sanitisers are provided in 150 locations in the park.
- Disinfection carpets were installed at the entrance of all the animal exhibition halls.
- All 'Kiss with Animals' activities were suspended.

7.2.1. Facility Cleaning and Disinfection

- The nano-photocatalyst coating is regularly applied to the main facilities, and cleaning and disinfection are conducted every 1–2 hours.
- All air-conditioning filters are sprayed with Bacterial Magic Thyme Disinfectant to kill 99% of viruses and bacteria.
- The cleaning team uses a high-pressure spray gun to deep clean the park every night.

7.2.2. Park Restaurants

- Tables are placed 1.5 m apart, and the maximum number of diners per table is limited to four.
- Catering facilities are thoroughly cleaned and sanitised before and after operations every day.
- Menus are cleaned and disinfected before opening, daily, and after each customer's use.
- Catering staff must wear a mask and gloves when handling food, and food is covered when transported from the kitchen to a table.

The relevant theme park in COVID-19 measures can be identified in [6, 7].

8. HONG KONG AIRPORT

Starting 1 August 2022, passengers were allowed to book a flight with a transit/transfer stop at the Hong Kong International Airport; however, they must have a valid air ticket or connecting boarding pass for a flight departing within 24 hours of their scheduled arrival time in Hong Kong. In addition, their luggage must be tagged for their next destination. All travellers must predetermine their entry at their final destination.

On 15 August 2020, passengers departing from airports in Mainland China were allowed to transit in/transfer to other destinations at the Hong Kong International Airport. However, transit/transfer services to various destinations in Mainland China remained suspended.

The sea-air transfer barge service from Shenzhen Shekou Port to Hong Kong International Airport Sky Ferry Terminal resumed operation on 23 March 2022. Clipper services from Mainland China and Macau ports to Sky Ferry Terminal remained suspended.

8.1. All Regions Except Mainland China, Macau and Taiwan

The regulations below are applicable to all Hong Kong and non-Hong Kong residents who have stayed/visited a city outside Mainland China, Macau, or Taiwan on the day of or 14 days before their boarding/arrival who have completed their vaccination doses and have an approved vaccination record.

8.1.1. Boarding Requirements

- Must present an approved vaccination record.
- Must present a certificate of a negative polymerase chain reaction (PCR) nucleic acid test taken within the last 48 hours before the scheduled departure time.
- Must present a booking confirmation for 7 nights (if the compulsory quarantine will be completed early after meeting the conditions) or 14 nights (if the compulsory quarantine will not be completed early) from a designated quarantine hotel.

8.1.2. Quarantine Requirements

- Must quarantine at a designated quarantine hotel for 14 days.
- Must take a rapid antigen test daily and a PCR nucleic acid test on the 3rd, 5th, 9th and 12th days during the compulsory quarantine period.

8.2. Mainland China and Macau

8.2.1. Boarding Requirements

- If vaccination is incomplete,
  - Must present a certificate of a negative PCR nucleic acid test on the day of scheduled arrival, taken within 3 days before the arrival date.
- If vaccination is complete,
  - Must present a certificate of a negative PCR nucleic acid test on the day of scheduled arrival, taken within 3 days before the arrival date.
  - Must present vaccination record.

8.2.2. Quarantine Requirements

- If vaccination is incomplete,
  - Must undergo 14-day compulsory quarantine at a designated location (home, hotel or other accommodation).
  - Must take two tests during the compulsory quarantine period (5th and 12th day of arrival in Hong Kong).
- If vaccination is complete,
  - Must undergo 7-day compulsory quarantine at a designated location (home, hotel or other accommodation).
  - Must take one test during the compulsory quarantine period (5th day of arrival in Hong Kong).
  - Must conduct self-monitoring for the succeeding 7 days.
  - Must conduct compulsory testing on the 12th day of arrival.

The relevant Hong Kong airport in COVID-19 measures can be found in [8].

9. SCHOOLS

On 19th May 2022, restrictions for students participating in half-day activities, such as graduation ceremonies, parents' day, opening day or campus visits, were relaxed. However, the students attending such events must comply with the pandemic prevention requirements of the different venues before entering.

Primary schools and kindergartens may arrange for students to participate in nonacademic extracurricular activities (*e.g.* music or sports activities and school team training) that do not require mask removal for half a day on Saturdays.

The 'Vaccination Pass' was implemented on 24 February 2022. All teaching and nonteaching staff of kindergartens, primary and secondary schools, and private schools that offer nonformal curricula (commonly referred to as 'tutorial schools'); persons who provide services on campus; and visitors are required to comply with the 'Vaccination Pass' requirements, except those who are exempted. On 20th March 2022, the government announced that it would adjust the vaccination requirements of the 'Vaccination Pass' (including a third dose of the vaccine) to further encourage the public to get vaccinated as soon as possible. Schools made corresponding arrangements, according to the relevant requirements.

- Teaching and non-teaching staff directly employed by a school must be vaccinated with a minimum number of doses, as follows:
- On or before 24 February 2022: first stitch.
- On or before 21 April 2022: second stitch.
- On or after 31 May 2022.
  - The second dose if less than 5 months after the second dose.
  - The third dose if 5 months after the second dose.

The relevant school in COVID-19 measures can be found in [9].

10. PUBLIC MARKETS

Body temperature detection systems or portable body temperature detection devices were installed or provided to measure the body temperature of the people entering the markets and hand sanitisers were placed in public areas such as elevator lobbies, escalators, and public spaces for customers. Market administrators reminded all market stall owners and citizens to wear a mask in the market area.

To improve air circulation in several markets, water-cooled portable air conditioners were purchased, according to actual needs. For example, ultraviolet disinfection devices were installed on escalator handrails in eight FEHD markets, including Wanchai Lockhart Road Market.

All FEHD markets posted the 'Safe Travel' QR code. The FEHD actively encouraged market tenants, stallholders, and the public to adopt contactless payment methods to reduce cash transactions and the risk of spreading the virus.

The FEHD installed automatic soap dispensers in street toilets and sensor-type toilet sanitisers in toilet cubicles.

Market management service contractors conduct a thorough cleaning and disinfection of every market every day after closing, using diluted household bleach. According to the situation of different markets in various districts, the FEHD arranged for the markets to close 1 hour earlier than regular closing hours every 3 months for regular deep cleaning, in response to the pandemic [10].

11. ELDERLY HOME

Visitors are required to have their body temperature checked before entering the premises, perform hand hygiene, and wear a surgical mask all the times during their visit. Residents must also wear a surgical mask and eye protection, when practical.

Residents must maintain a social distance of 1 m.

Rooms, kitchens, toilets and bathrooms must be kept clean and hygienic. Specifically, 1:99 diluted household bleach must be used for cleaning and disinfection, and metal surfaces must be cleaned and disinfected with 70% alcohol.

The fresh air supply must be sufficient if air-conditioning equipment are used in the residential care home. The staff must ensure that the air-conditioning equipment are functioning properly.

The dust filters of air-conditioning equipment must be cleaned regularly.

The body temperature of all the residents must be checked daily for early detection of those with a fever (oral probe: temperature above 37.5 °C; ear probe: temperature above 38 °C).

Residents must wear a patch and surgical mask if they have a fever or respiratory infection symptoms or experience sudden loss of taste/smell. The staff must arrange for residents with such symptoms to seek medical treatment as soon as possible.

The staff must check their body temperature before going to work and must stay home if they have a fever or respiratory infection symptoms or experience a sudden loss of taste/smell and seek medical attention and notify the institution immediately.

When residents go to their hometown for vacation, under special circumstances, they must notify the residential institution of their return. The staff must record their contact history whilst on vacation and observe their physical condition. Isolation and detection practices must be continued according to the risk assessment.

Residential homes must take prudent and effective measures to reduce the risk of infection, including limiting the number of visitors to avoid gathering crowds in the hospital and the number of visitors per resident to a maximum of one at a time. Visitors must have at least two doses of the COVID-19 vaccine and present their vaccination record to the institution and take a COVID-19 rapid antigen test at a designated location in the institution before their visit, with a negative result. Visits must be limited to designated locations, with appropriate barriers and frequent disinfection. The home must ensure that all visitors comply with the relevant requirements and keep a visitor record [11].

12. CHURCH

For Congregants:

a. Must bring their own personal effects, if needed (*e.g.* prayer rugs or scriptures).
b. Must check their body temperature before visiting; those with a fever or respiratory infection symptoms should cancel their visit, wear a surgical mask and seek medical attention immediately.
c. Must wear a mask when attending religious gatherings, wash their hands before entering the premises and maintain vigilance and good personal hygiene, such as washing their hands after attending gatherings.
d. Must avoid physical contact and maintain a social distance of at least 1 m from one another.

Physical Setting:

a. Religious ceremonies and activities should be conducted through live broadcasts or other online media platforms.
b. If online/virtual gatherings are not feasible, the meeting time should be shortened, and the number of congregants should be limited to reduce contact between the participants.
c. Religious gatherings may be held in small groups to ensure adequate social distancing among the congregants.
d. Body temperature checks are conducted at the entrance to the premises. Employees must wear a surgical mask, take the temperature of the congregants at the entrance, and deny entry to those with a fever.
e. Adequate hand hygiene facilities must be provided at entrances and within the premises, such as hand sanitisers containing 70%–80% alcohol. Masks should be provided to those in need.
f. The number of worshippers entering the premises, participating in the activities and leaving the premises must be controlled, and a social distance of at least 1 m should be maintained as much as possible.

The relevant church in COVID-19 measures can be found in [12].

13. MUSEUMS

Museums reopened on 21 April 2022, for a limited number of visitors. Individuals entering sports arenas or other indoor premises managed by the LCSD must comply with the relevant requirements of the 'Vaccination Pass'. Visitors are also required to undergo temperature checks and use alcohol-based hand sanitisers before entering a venue and wear a mask at all times. All venues should strengthen their cleaning and disinfection measures.

All performance venues (except Tai Po Civic Centre, Sheung Wan Civic Centre and Sai Wan Ho Civic Centre) resumed their hosting of performances and/or events with live audiences on April 21, with special seating arrangements. In the main facilities of such venues, such as concert halls, theatres, performance halls, cultural entertainment halls and performance venues, the number of spectators should not exceed half of the original capacity, and the number of consecutive occupied seats should not exceed four. Performers who are unable to wear a mask during rehearsals or performances must take a government-approved COVID-19 reverse transcription PCR nucleic acid test within 7 days before their first performance and have a certificate of a negative rapid antigen test.

For activities/events held in activity and conference rooms, the number of users should not exceed half of the original capacity. Furthermore, eating and drinking are prohibited in rented facilities [13].

14. HONG KONG COLISEUM

- On 19 May 2022, the restriction on the number of audience seats was relaxed to 85% (*i.e.* 10,625, but subject to the number of seats and arrangement of individual programs), but the number of consecutive occupied seats must not exceed eight.
- Eating and drinking are prohibited in rental facilities.
- All users/spectators must wear a mask before entering the venue.
- Body temperature must be checked when entering the venue; visitors must clean their hands with 70%–80% alcohol-based hand sanitiser.
- Visitors must comply with the relevant requirements of the 'Vaccination Pass' and use their mobile phone to scan the 'Safe Travel' QR code.
- All public events on the fairgrounds remain suspended.

The relevant Hong Kong Coliseum COVID-19 measure can be available in [14].

15. PUBLIC TRANSPORTATION

15.1. MTR

In addition to cleaning and sterilising the station with 1:99 diluted bleach (every 2 hours), a 'hydrogen atomising robot' automatically sprays hydrogen peroxide, atomised to a specific concentration, for additional deep cleaning and disinfection. The nano-photocatalyst coating is also applied, which can continuously eliminate a variety of bacteria and viruses for 2 to 3 years.

Disinfection stations are set up in all stations to provide passengers with disinfectant hand sanitisers. The stations also strengthened their fresh air intake system to improve indoor air circulation. The MTR authority installed automatic sensors on hundreds of lifts for noncontact operation to reduce the spread of the virus [15].

15.2. Buses

For Employees

1. The vehicle control centre implemented temperature checks for all frontline employees, vehicle captains and external cleaning staff, using infrared heat detectors.

2. Masks are provided for employees on duty.

3. Hand sanitisers are provided in the stationmaster's room and bus captains' lounge in major bus terminals.

4. Transparent plastic sheets were installed in staff canteens, 24-hour vehicle control centres and so on to avoid the spread of the virus through droplets.

5. Appropriate arrangements were made for office staff to work from home to reduce crowd gathering.

The fully automatic air-conditioning system installed in bus compartments will draw in the outside air through its fresh air function, which will be filtered by the system to reduce the impact of outside exhaust air on the passengers. In addition, cabin air-conditioning systems are equipped with a dust filter and an electrostatic air-cleaning device.

Circulation was strengthened in bus compartments, and the air in cabins is filtered through the ionisation effect, which can effectively reduce the particle and bacteria level in the compartment.

After bus operations for the day, cleaners use 1:99 diluted bleach to clean and disinfect the cabin and cab. The air-conditioning system dust filters are dismantled and cleaned by engineers no less than twice a month, using diluted bleach [16].

CONCLUSION

To sum up, this chapter mainly addresses the main anti-epidemic measures adopted by the local community. A total of 14 examples are highlighted to demonstrate the various measures adopted owing to the COVID-19 pandemic. Actual photos of the detailed measures are also presented. Anti-epidemic measures can significantly affect people's lives and daily routines to a certain extent. This chapter may provide valuable insights into global post-COVID-19-pandemic measures.

REFERENCES

[1]   Leisure and cultural services department. HKSAR Sports Centre 2022. Available from:https://www.lcsd.gov.hk/en/facilities/facilitieslist/landsports/sportcentre.html

[2]   Hospital Authority HKSAR. 2022. Available from: https://www.ha.org.hk/visitor/ha_index.asp?Lang=CHIB5

[3]   Leisure and Cultural Services Department . HKSAR. Beaches and Swimming Pools. 2022. Available from: https://www.lcsd.gov.hk/en/beach/swim-intro/swim-location-hk.html

[4]   Food and Environmental Hygiene Department . HKSAR. 2022. Available from: https://www.fehd.gov.hk/english/events/covid19/vaccine_bubble_faq_banquet.html

[5]   South CMP. Coronavirus: Scramble for gym, cinema sessions hours before hong kong's leisure venue ban as part of social distancing kicks in. 2022. Available from: https://www.scmp.com/news/hong-kong/health-environment/article/3077404/coronavirus-scramble-gym-cinema-sessions-hours

[6]   Disneyland HK. 2022. Available from: https://www.hongkongdisneyland.com/zh-hk/

[7]   Hong KOP. 2022. Available from: https://ticketing.oceanpark.com.hk/oceanpark_b2c/ticketselection.html?utm_source=google&utm_medium=cpc&utm_campaign=EG_SEM_DP&gclid=EAIaIQobChMI492Ql5KkgAMVjzVgCh0vMg6SEAAYASAAEgIfIfD_BwE

[8]   Hong Kong International Airport. 2022. Available from: https://www.hongkongairport.com/en/passenger-guide/COVID19.page

[9]   Education Bureau. 2022. Available from: https://www.edb.gov.hk/en/sch-admin/admin/about-sch/diseases-prevention/index.html

[10] Food and Environmental Hygiene Department. 2022. Available from: https://www.fehd.gov.hk/english/index.html

[11] Social Welfare Department. 2022. Available from:https://www.swd.gov.hk/en/index/site_pubsvc/page_lr/sub_covid19info/

[12] Catholic Diocese of Hong Kong. 2022. Available from: https://catholic.org.hk/en/cn20220118/

[13] World A. Hong kong museums shut down for the third time after yet another new spike in infections 2020. Available from: https://news.artnet.com/art-world/hong-kong-museums-shutter-third-time-1894516

[14] Coliseum HK. Leisure and cultural services department, HKSAR. 2022. Available from:

https://www.lcsd.gov.hk/en/hkc/

[15]   MTR. 2022. Available from: https://www.mtr.com.hk/en/customer/main/COVID-19-precaution-report.html

[16]   Legislative Council Secretariat. HKSAR. COVID-19 epidemic's impacts on transport sector. 2021. Available from: https://www.legco.gov.hk/research-publications/english/2021issh27-covid-19-epidemics-impacts-on-transport-sector-20210603-e.pdf

CHAPTER 6

Homes for the Aged in the COVID-19 Pandemic

Abstract: In the context of the COVID-19 pandemic, homes for the aged have seriously suffered from the fifth wave of COVID-19. Although the problem of an ageing population emerges as a global issue, the relevant studies related to homes for the aged are under-researched. In this chapter, we explored the weaknesses of homes for the aged and weak government policies that have posed threats to homes for the aged to deal with numerous confirmed cases of COVID-19. In response, we propose possible ways for homes for the aged to deal with the challenges arising from the COVID-19 pandemic. It may give useful guidelines for the policymakers, researchers, homes for the aged, and the local community to design and implement anti-epidemic measures in the forthcoming years.

Keywords: Ageing population, Homes for the aged, The fifth wave of the COVID-19 pandemic.

1. INTRODUCTION

In recent years, the problem of the ageing population has become a global issue. According to the research, in 2019, the global population aged 65 years or over was around 703 million. In 2050, it is estimated that the population will increase to 1.5 billion [1]. It is unavoidable that Hong Kong is also facing the same challenge. Starting in 1963, the birth rate in Hong Kong has been decreasing. From 1963 to 2020, the birth rate decreased by around 62% [2]. While the birth rate is dropping, life expectancy in Hong Kong keeps on increasing. In 1981, the life expectancy of men and women was 72.3 and 78.5, respectively. In 2020, it increased to 83.4 and 87.7, respectively [3]. Since life expectancy has increased, it shows the death rate in Hong Kong has become lower. Owing to the decreasing birth rate and increasing life expectancy, the ageing population problem has become more serious in Hong Kong. It causes a common problem: the shortage of subsidized residential care places for the elderly.

From the data of the World Bank, we can find that the number of populations aged 65 and above increased 15.7 times from 1960 to 2020 [4]. The great number of elderly leads to a greater demand for elderly homes. According to the Labour and Welfare Bureau, starting from 2017 to 2018, the supply of subsidized residen-

Yui-yip Lau, Tang Yuk Ming & Leung Wai Keung Alan

tial care places for the elderly increased by 584. However, at the same time, the demand for the places increased by 7681 [5]. It means that even though the supply of subsidized residential care places increased, it still cannot cover the increase in demand. Although the Hong Kong government tried to increase the supply of the places, the result is that the waiting time only decreased from 25-37 months (in 2013) to 19 months (2021) [6]. It shows that the shortage problem is still serious today.

2. THE PROBLEMS ARISING FROM HOMES FOR THE AGED DURING COVID-19 PANDEMIC

First, as mentioned before, there is a serious shortage of subsidized residential care places. Therefore, most of the elderly would choose to live in private residential care places. Facing the great demand, most private residential care places face a problem of labour shortage. According to a document from the Social Welfare Advisory Committee, in the high-care level residential care homes (RCH), the ratio of care workers and the elderly is 1:20 during the daytime; for the nighttime, the ratio becomes 1:40. For the medium care level RCH, the ratio is 1:30 while the ratio of Registered Nurse (RN) and the elderly is 1:60 [7]. The data shows that the manpower of private RCH has a significant shortage. The shortage means it is impossible for the care workers to take care of every elderly carefully and attentively and keep the workplace clear at any time. Therefore, under COVID-19, the shortage of manpower become one of the main reasons for the spread of the virus quickly.

Second, there is a shortage of protective equipment. At the beginning of the fifth wave, most of the private RCHs did not prepare enough equipment for their care workers. Care workers belong to high-exposure work. Therefore, if the workers do not have good Personal Protective Equipment (PPE) to protect themselves, they easily get the pandemic from others. And then, since the incubation period range of COVID-19 is 1 to 14 days, during the incubation, the workers can spread the virus to the elderly [3]. Besides, most of the care workers in RCH do not have a high educational level. As such, it is possible that they do not have enough knowledge on how to prevent the spread of the epidemic or use PPE correctly. These can cause the breakout of COVID-19 in the RCHs.

Third, the space of RCH is too small which is advantageous for the spread of COVID-19. According to the Labour and Welfare Bureau, the minimum area of floor space for each resident in RCH is 6.5 m^2 [8]. Living in a crowded area, it is easier to spread the epidemic. Besides, because of the limited space, it is hard for the RCH to separate the patient and the others with a suitable distance and space. Therefore, as an airborne disease, COVID-19 can spread in this tiny area.

3. THE POSSIBLE WAYS FOR HOMES FOR THE AGED DURING THE COVID-19 PANDEMIC

To solve the aforementioned problems, some solutions are recommended.

First, of the lack of care workers problem, it is encouraged that the salary should be enhanced. For the subsidized RCH, the average starting salary point is $12,349 and the average maximum salary point is $14,703 [9]. The average salary in Hong Kong is over $17,000 [10]. It can be found that the salary for working as a care worker for subsidized RCH has already been low. For the private RCH, since they do not get a subsidy from the government, the salary could be lower. The workload of care workers is very high, especially for the medium/low care level RCH. As such, low salary is hard to attract people to enter this industry. Thus, the vacancy rate remains high. Besides, the government can set some programmes to attract mainland care workers to work for Hong Kong RCH. To attract them, the Hong Kong government can offer some benefits on taxes and housing. Since the rent in Hong Kong is very high, facing the high rent, most non-local workers are not willing to work in Hong Kong. Under low salaries and high rent, the existing programme is hard to attract mainland care workers to work in Hong Kong. Therefore, if the government want to enhance the manpower in the care worker market, it should improve the working condition.

Second, for the shortage of equipment, whether RCH is subsidized or not, they should prepare enough PPE for the unforeseeable situation. Besides, the government can offer some short-term courses to the RCH workers to teach them how to use the equipment correctly, what they should do during the outbreak and how to prevent the outbreak.

Third, the government should improve the relative law. For example, the minimum area of floor space for each resident is significantly not enough. The government should increase the floor space and stipulate the space of the common area. Further, the government can also set up a standard for the air ventilation assessment register so that it can reduce the possibility of airborne transmission when there is a pandemic.

CONCLUSION

In this section, we mainly propose possible ways for homes for the aged during the COVID-19 pandemic. To solve the aforementioned problems, some solutions are recommended.

REFERENCES

[1]   United Nations. World Population Ageing 2019: Highlights. 2019. Available from: https://www.un.org/en/development/desa/population/publications/pdf/ageing/WorldPopulationAgeing 2019-Highlights.pdf

[2]   Public Health Information System. Birth Rate. 2022. Available from: https://www.healthyhk.gov.hk/phisweb/en/chart_detail/14/

[3]   Men's Facts - Life Expectancy at Birth. 2022. Available from: https://www.chp.gov.hk/tc/index.html

[4]   The World Bank. Population ages 65 and above, total - Hong Kong SAR, China. 2021. Available from: https://data.worldbank.org/indicator/SP.POP.65UP.TO?locations=HK

[5]   Labour and Welfare Bureau. Progress in Elderly Services: Residential Services. 2021. Available from: https://www.lwb.gov.hk/tc/blog/post_12122021.html

[6]   HKSAR. LCQ14: Subsidised residential care places for elderly and persons with disabilities. 2013. Available from: https://www.info.gov.hk/gia/general/201302/27/P201302270287.htm

[7]   Social Welfare Advisory Committee. Call for Improved Care for the Elderly. 2020. Available from: https://www.districtcouncils.gov.hk/tm/doc/2020_2023/tc/committee_meetings_doc/ssc/18425/ssc_20 20_027.pdf

[8]   Hong Kong e-Legislation. Cap. 459A Residential Care Homes (Elderly Persons) Regulation. 2020. Available   from: https://www.elegislation.gov.hk/hk/cap459A!en?INDEX_CS=N&pmc=0&m=0&pm=1

[9]   HKSAR. LCQ7: Manpower shortage in elderly service sector. 2017. Available from: https://www.info.gov.hk/gia/general/201711/29/P2017112900367.htm?fontSize=1

[10] Economics T. Hong Kong Average Monthly Salaries. 2022. Available from: https://tradingeconomics.com/hong-kong/wages

CHAPTER 7

The Adoption of Mobile App for the Elderly in the 21st Century

Abstract: In general, the elderly mainly face two kinds of problems, namely physical and mental. Such kinds of problems lead to the unfolded challenges for the elderly in the community. Also, it may increase the burden on the healthcare system in the long term. To this end, this chapter introduces the adoption of mobile apps for the elderly to increase the elderly social mobility and mitigate the overloaded public healthcare system in the future.

Keywords: Healthcare system, Mental problem, Physical problem, Social mobility, The elderly.

1. INTRODUCTION

1.1. The Challenges for the Elderly in Society

In recent years, the problem of the ageing population hits the headlines. According to the survey, in 2038, the elderly population (65 years old and above) will increase to 2.44 million [1]. Because of the ageing population, more and more people are concerned about the life quality of the elderly. When people become elderly, it is unavoidable that they will face different problems and difficulties in their daily lives. These can be separated into 2 main aspects: physical problems and mental problems.

1.1.1. Physical Problems of the Elderly

First, for physical problems, when a human becomes older, their somatic function would be worse than before. For example, the elderly always face visual challenges, verbal challenges, aural challenges and mental challenges. According to the report from Hong Kong Blind Union, in 2021, there are 199,600 people with visual impairment. The majority of the people (73.5%) are aged 60 or above [2]. In 2018, over 150 000 people were suffering from verbal challenges and more than 80% of them are elderly [3]. In 2017, there were around 100,000 people which is one-tenth of the elderly population suffering from dementia [4]. These challenges can affect the daily life of the elderly and their quality of life becomes

Yui-yip Lau, Tang Yuk Ming & Leung Wai Keung Alan

lower. For instance, the elderly cannot see things clearly, so it is hard for them to read newspapers or some traditional entertainment. Also, verbal challenge means the elderly cannot hear clearly. Besides, the elderly suffering from dementia would be forgetful and their behaviour change to be more aggressive [5]. In fact, in recent years, many accidents are happening to the elderly because of dementia. There are research works that show that over 30% of the respondents said their family members who suffer from dementia have experienced getting lost [6]. Having bad memory not only causes the elderly to get lost easily but also make them prone to home accidents. For example, when the elderly are cooking, they may forget to turn off the fire and go away to do another thing. If the elderly keeps forgetting to turn off the fire, it can be on fire. Thus, we can find that when people become older, their physical ability become weaker. It can bring a great negative influence on their quality of life.

1.1.2. Mental Problems of the Elderly

Second, mental problems, because of weaker physical ability, can make the elderly to suffer from some mood disorders. Mood disorder is "a disorder in which you experience long periods of extreme happiness, extreme sadness, or both. Certain mood disorders involve other persistent emotions, such as anger and irritability." [7]. In fact, in Hong Kong, one out of 10 elderly experience depressive symptoms and 4.7% of people aged 66-75 suffer from depression. Besides, for the suicide cases in 2015, 30% of the cases were aged 65 or above [8]. The data shows that there are a number of elderly who have mental problems. The main reason for the elderly is mental illness. According to the World Health Organization (WHO), facing health problems (*e.g.*, reduced mobility, chronic pain, frailty) or serious illness (*e.g.*, heart disease) is one of the main factors for mental health problems in the elderly [9].

2. MOBILE APP FOR THE ELDERLY

To improve the quality of life for the elderly, it is suggested that we make use of a new mobile app to help the elderly face the problems mentioned above.

In a Digital City, how to make use of technology to improve the life quality of life has become a significant topic of interest. According to the survey, in 2019, the penetration rate of smartphones was 91.5% and 2 out of 3 people aged 65 or above owned smartphones [10]. Based on the data, it shows the possibility that we can design a new app for the elderly to improve their quality of life by solving the problems mentioned above.

The functions of the app can be separated into 3 main aspects.

First, the elderly can communicate with doctors and social workers using the app. Telemedicine is useful to the elderly, especially disabled persons. It is because it is hard for the elderly to walk a long way to see a doctor. Besides, it can minimize the possibility that the elderly have some accidents when they go to the hospital/clinic. Although telemedicine is developed in many countries, in Hong Kong, during COVID-19, people just find the importance of telemedicine and start to develop it. However, since this industry is developing during COVID-19, most of the apps or websites that offer the function of telemedicine are only for people suffering from COVID-19. It means in Hong Kong, the service coverage of telemedicine is not big enough. One of the examples is HA Go. It was launched by the Hospital Authority. Although the user can make a booking for telemedicine by using the app, the user must be a COVID-19 user [11]. The new app can cooperate with some private clinics, especially with some clinics which can use the elderly health care voucher to pay the fee. Several elderlies are not willing to see doctors when they get ill because they do not know which clinic can use the voucher and so they think that seeing a doctor is wasting money. By using the app, the elderly can directly find the clinic which can use the voucher and reduce the time spent on going hospital/clinic. The app can make the elderly see the doctor more conveniently. Thus, it can enhance the willingness of the elderly to find a doctor when they feel sick. In other words, if the elderly get some serious illness, it can help the elderly do some early detection and prevention. For the social worker, the elderly can find social workers by using the app. For the disabled elderly, it is hard for them to visit the workers' office frequently. To a certain extent, it is also impossible for the workers to visit the elderly every day. It means it is quite inconvenient for the elderly when they want to get help from the workers or even just want to talk with the workers. To improve the efficiency of the visiting of social workers, it is better to get meetings online. By using the app, the elderly and the social workers can communicate when they want. It can help to reduce the possibility of suicide since it can help the worker to notice mental problems in the elderly on time.

Second, the app can check the heart rate of the elderly and when necessary, it can help to call the police. Because of the development of technology, when there is a smartphone, there is no need to use a smartwatch or other equipment to check the heart rate. Through making use of photoplethysmography, the elderly only need to put their finger on the built-in camera of the phone and then the app will "measure your heart rate by detecting changes in blood volume below the skin's surface" [12]. Since not all the elderly own a sphygmomanometer at home, this function can help the elderly get a record of their heart rate frequently. Thus, if the elderly suffer from some heart disease, it can give an alert to the elderly and connect with telemedicine so that the elderly can get treatment as early as possible.

Third, the app has a global positioning system (GPS). It means when the elderly get lost somewhere, the family members or carers can make use of the GPS to find the elderly. Moreover, since the GPS is linked to the map when the elderly want to go some places that they do not know how to go, the app can teach them the way. Also, the target customers of the app are the elderly. In doing so, the design of the app would be user-friendly for the elderly. For example, if the elderly face visual challenges, the app offers the option of voice navigation. In addition, the font size of the app would be larger than the normal app so that the elderly can read the word more easily.

Although all the functions mentioned above or similar functions can be found in the existing apps, just like HA Go, services offered by the Senior Citizen Home Safety Association and Google Maps. However, none of them owns a great function coverage. Although the penetration rate of smartphones is high, it does not mean the elderly are good at using a smartphone. To this end, if there is an app that can offer all the necessary and useful functions to the elderly, it would be of great convenience for them in their daily routine.

CONCLUSION

Although all the functions mentioned above or similar functions can be found in the existing apps, just like HA Go, services offered by the Senior Citizen Home Safety Association and Google Maps. However, none of them owns a great function coverage. Although the penetration rate of smartphones is high, it does not mean the elderly are good at using a smartphone. To this end, if there is an app that can offer all the necessary and useful functions to the elderly, it would be more convenient for them in their daily life.

REFERENCES

[1]   Wong K, Yeung M. Population ageing trends of Hong Kong. Hong Kong: Office of the Government Economist, The Government of the Hong Kong Special Administrative Region 2019. Available from: https://www.hkeconomy.gov.hk/en/pdf/el/el-2019-02.pdf

[2]   Hong Kong Blind Union. Statistics on People with Visual Impairment. 2021. Available from: https://www.hkbu.org.hk/en/knowledge/statistics/index

[3]   HKSAR. LCQ13: Assisting the deaf/hard-of-hearing residents in residential care homes for the elderly. 2018. Available from: https://www.info.gov.hk/gia/general/201806/13/P2018061300406.htm

[4]   Health Bureau. Mental Health Review Report. 2017. Available from: https://www.healthbureau.gov.hk/download/press_and_publications/otherinfo/180500_mhr/e_mhr_full_report.pdf

[5]   The Elderly Health Service. 2020. Available from: https://www.elderly.gov.hk/english/common_health_problems/dementia/dementia.html

[6]   Jockey Club Centre for Positive Ageing. The Latest Online Survey Found that More Than 30% of People with Dementia Have Been Lost and Nearly 80% of Caregivers are Worried About Their Family Members Will Be Lost Again. Electronic Tracking Devices Have Become a Major Trend. 2021. Available from: https://www.jccpa.org.hk/wp-content/uploads/2021/10/CCD_Survey-Resu-t-Press-Release.pdf

[7]   Cleveland Clinic. Mood Disorders: What They Are, Symptoms & Treatment. 2022. Available from: https://my.clevelandclinic.org/health/diseases/17843-mood-disorders

[8]   HKSAR. World Health Day 2017 calls for concern about depression (with photos). 2017. Available from: https://www.info.gov.hk/gia/general/201704/07/P2017040700174.htm?fontSize=1

[9]   World Health Organization. Mental health of older adults 2017. Available from: https://www.who.int/news-room/fact-sheets/detail/mental-health-of-older-adults

[10]   HKSAR. Thematic Household Survey Report No. 69 published. 2019. Available from: https://www.info.gov.hk/gia/general/202003/26/P2020032600444.htm?fontSize=1

[11]   Hospital Authority. Book Tele/DC. 2021. Available from: https://www2.ha.org.hk/hago/en/features/appointment-related/book-dc

[12]   Kosecki D. How to track your heart rate with only your smartphone. 2019. Available from: https://www.cnet.com/health/how-to-track-your-heart-rate-with-a-smartphone/

CHAPTER 8

Narrative Review of Mobile Technology: Evidence from Older Adults

Abstract: In the 21st century, many developed countries have become aging societies. Although network speed, the improvement of smartphones, and 5G foster the growth of mobile technology, the employment of mobile technology exhibited a significant gap in the design and application of mobile technology that can be applied for older adults. This study analyses the design and implementation of mobile technologies to investigate novel mobile applications that support older adults in aged homes, by conducting a comprehensive discussion. As such, this study selects an expert narrative overview of a literature search from Google Scholar and archives. Analysis results reveal that designing new mobile apps, strengthening the interaction through VR technologies, and developing smartwatches for nursing homes. We need to consult older adults to ascertain if they are willing to use the technology. Mobile technology provides better support for older adults and monitors their health condition.

Keywords: Aging societies, Mobile technology, Mobile application, Older adults.

1. INTRODUCTION

Mobile technologies have played a significant role in our daily lives in recent years. The network speed, 5G, and the enhancement of smartphones stimulate the growth of mobile technology [1, 2]. The adoption of mobile technology has been widely used in both professional and personal activities [3]. With the use of technology, many tasks are simplified and become more efficient while lacking manpower. "Mobile devices are increasingly being used to extend the human mind's limited capacity to recall and process large numbers of relevant variables to support information management, general administration, and clinical practice" [4]. Some activities are performed through a mobile platform and eliminate geographical constraints. In other words, mobile technology fosters free living, communication, and social participation anywhere and anytime [5]. Mobile phone usage in Asia is growing as shown by more than 50% of the Asian population employing smartphones [6].

The operational issues faced by aged homes are becoming more serious in Hong Kong. Three key issues are being identified, including the lack of mobile apps designed for older adults, social isolation of older adults, and the demand exceeding the supply of elderly nursing services [2]. Lee *et al.* [7] defined older adults commonly described as those aged 65 or above. In general, older adults are identified as less knowledgeable compared with younger generations. They are unfamiliar with software and operating systems and have weak operational skills, such as clicking and scrolling [8]. Some older adults recognized themselves as being 'too old' to understand how to adopt the technology. This indicates a higher degree of technological uneasiness and suffering from frustrations associated with the use of communication technology [10, 11]. As such, designing and implementing mobile technologies to improve the situation is not being paid enough attention and is poorly addressed. With the advancement of mobile technology, there exists a significant gap in the design and application of mobile technology that can be used for older adults, especially in Hong Kong.

The newly developed mobile technology is common among general patients but is not recognized by older adults. Nevertheless, older adults are presently digitally conscious because of their demand to keep in contact with family or friends, search for information, and have good communication [12]. Mobile technology is crucial to fulfilling the demand for active aging. Lee *et al.* [7] highlighted that "older adults were found to be more mobile today than in the past". Thus, mobile devices have come to be increasingly significant in daily life, even if highly complicated for older adult users. The user interface and the approaches to designing the mobile for this group must be distinct from the young generation [1]. Mobile technology is a technology designed to increase, maintain, or improve the functional capabilities of people with disabilities, older adults, or people with chronic health conditions [8, 2].

This provides a viewpoint and produces a technical paper for healthcare specialists, researchers, aged homes, clinicians, industry practitioners, and technology developers. A comprehensive search for the related scientific literature was conducted by adopting different scientific databases, such as SpringerLink, Google Scholar, EBSCO Host, and Science Direct. The scope of the publication of the literature review is the use of mobile technology for older adults. We focus on homes for the aged in Hong Kong since Hong Kong is now facing a serious aging problem. To the best of the authors' knowledge, there is a serious lack of research studies relevant to older adults, notably the application of mobile technology for older adults. Further, the social context of Hong Kong's homes for the aged industry is booming. Some key issues of older adults are still not yet solved.

The rest of this paper is structured as follows. Section 2 presents operational issues of homes for the aged. The recommendations and solutions to the issues are represented and discussed in Section 3. Section 4 provides a conclusion and direction for future research.

2. KEY OPERATIONAL ISSUES

Mobile technology is one of the assistive technologies [8, 9, 13]. With the emergence of 5G, smartphone improvement, and the advancement of mobile technology, the design and application of mobile technology for older adults have exhibited a significant research gap. Thus, this study addresses how design principles and device features of mobile technology reduce the gap between the demands of older adults and their needs. To what extent are older adults considered in the mobile App design process? How does the design and implementation of mobile technology foster older adults to access smart cities?

2.1. Lack of Mobile Apps Focused on Older Adult Needs

In 2019, the global population reached 703 million. The higher living standard, advanced medical treatment, and availability of nutrient-rich foods further extended the global average life expectancy. In this sense, the number of older adults is estimated to double to 1.5 million before 2050 [7]. Many developed countries have come to be aging societies [12]. The aging population in Hong Kong is growing at a substantial rate. Hong Kong is concerned that the older adult population rate will be growing from 17.9% to 31.9% between 2018 and 2038 (Fig. **1**). In 2038, almost one in three people will be older [14].

Given the aging population structure in modern society, mobile phone users are not limited to only young and middle-aged people but also older adults. According to the Hong Kong Census and Statistics Department [15], there was a certainly noticeable increase in the usage of smartphones among older adults. The coverage rate of owning smartphones increased from 6.9% in 2012 to 57.2% in 2019 (Table **1**). This proves that the demand for older adults for mobile phones has increased.

Smartphones are smart devices with many functions and applications, such as logging in to social media, making phone calls, and setting alarm clocks. However, complicated functions may be difficult for older adults. This is because many older people have no experience using computers, related software, and applications. Therefore, there is a significant gap in knowledge and expertise among this group, creating obstacles to adopting electronic equipment. Some older adults lack confidence in learning and operating smartphones. Older adults are not as easy and fast as younger generations learn to use technology products [16].

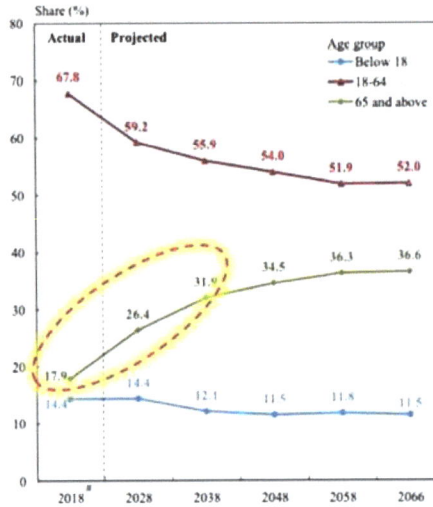

Fig. (1). The population of Hong Kong by age group from 2018 to 2066.

Table 1. Persons aged 10 and over had smartphones by age/sex, number of persons ('000).

Age Group/Sex	Survey Period				
	Jun-Aug 2012	May-Aug 2015	Jun-Sep 2017	Jun-Sep 2018	Apr-Jul 2019
10-14	140.3	201.1	214.5	220.3	237.4
-	(46.1%)	(76.9%)	(81.3%)	(81.1%)	(81.3%)
15-24	678.6	760.5	723.1	698.2	673.1
-	(80.3%)	(97.9%)	(99.5%)	(99.4%)	(99.6%)
25-34	830.9	951.4	954.7	935.5	940.00
-	(87.0%)	(98.8%)	(99.8%)	(99.8%)	(99.9%)
35-44	782.2	1002.4	1018.1	1031.1	1029.9
-	(74.5%)	(97.5%)	(99.4%)	(99.6%)	(99.7%)
45-54	637.6	1110.3	119.6	1108.2	1103.3
-	(51.5%)	(93.4%)	(97.8%)	(98.7%)	(99.3%)
55-64	262.9	871.1	1053.4	1122.0	1165.8
-	(27.4%)	(81.0%)	(92.5%)	(94.7%)	(96.5%)
≥65	63.3	373.9	604.8	696.2	824.0
-	(6.9%)	(35.4%)	(52.1%)	(57.2%)	(65.1%)

Source: Hong Kong Census and Statistics Department [15].

There are many health-related mobile phone applications, but few are designed for older adults. In addition, very few mobile phone applications are completely tailored for older adult users in the market. Most applications are complicated and have sole functions that are not convenient for older adult users [2].

There are three illustrative examples of complicated applications based on constructive advice from health specialists and homes for the aged. First, the e-See Find App has the main function to let relatives and friends check the approximate location of older adults. The drawbacks of this application are inaccurate and low functionality. Second, the MyTherapy Pill Reminder App is a reminder to consume medicine or measure blood pressure regularly. It also provides a real-time alert for other family members. However, its usage method is complicated. Third, the Senior Citizen Card App provides information on preferential goods and services such as diet, clinics, and Chinese medicine. Low update frequency is the drawback of this application [16, 17].

Older adults need to download many different applications and learn to use them one by one. Older adults also do not know how to search for health-related information on the internet. Most mobile phone application developers are young people. They seldom think about the user needs from the older adult's perspective, leading to the application functions that do not meet the needs of older adults [17].

The challenge for the aged care industry is that the demand for the elderly nursing service market is increasing, but the labor force is limited [18]. Although mobile technologies such as smartphones, smartwatches, and tablet computers are increasingly used to collect data and monitor different situations to reduce the workload of the staff, the implementation is not enough to resolve the problem [19].

2.2. Older Adults' Social Isolation

Social isolation is "the objective quantitative reduction in a person's social network and several contacts" [20]. Older adults are one of the groups affected by social isolation. Social isolation is also one of the driving forces for generating suicide risk in older adults [6]. Moving to aged homes significantly changes older adults' social lives and interactions with their friends and families. Lack of social interaction can be commonly seen in aged homes. Although the facilities and care are undoubtedly exceptional nowadays, some older adults still feel lonely and socially isolated. In 2020, persons aged 65 or above who used the internet during the 12 months before enumeration was 62.2% from April to July 2019 (Table **2**). 62.2% of older adults used information technology and the internet, while 47.8% did not know how to access the Internet. However, some older adults with disabilities and age-old were unable to use smartphones and computers. These make them socially isolated, leading them to a lack of communication, homesickness, and being behind the times [16, 17].

Table 2. Persons aged 10 or above used the internet during the 12 months before enumeration by age/sex, number of persons ('000).

Age Group/Sex	Survey Period				
	Apr-Jun 2001	Jun-Aug 2009	Jun-Aug 2014	Apr-Jul 2016	Apr-Jul 2019
10-14	341.2	369.3	267.7	251.2	292.2
-	(79.4%)	(98.8%)	(99.4%)	(99.7%)	(100.0%)
15-24	743.0	849.3	801.7	762.4	675.4
-	(81.1%)	(99.1%)	(99.6%)	(99.8%)	(99.9%)
25-34	717.1	903.3	951.2	959.1	940.30
-	(65.1%)	(95.2%)	(99.0%)	(99.6%)	(100%)
35-44	574.0	947.9	994.0	1009.9	1030.9
-	(42.3%)	(85.6%)	(96.6%)	(99.5%)	(99.8%)
45-54	189.8	852.0	1066.9	1136.9	1103.7
-	(19.6%)	(67.5%)	(88.2%)	(97.3%)	(99.3%)
55-64	29.8	304.1	728.7	971.8	1158.8
-	(6.0%)	(37.9%)	(69.9%)	(87.7%)	(95.9%)
≥65	6.2	74.0	242.2	486.2	786.7
-	(0.8%)	(8.8%)	(24.0%)	(44.0%)	(62.2%)

Source: National Institute on Aging [21].

2.2.1. Communication Lacking and Homesickness

There are few social interactions in the home for the aged except for meeting other older adults. Moving older adults to aged homes makes them unable to meet their friends and family, making them feel lonely. Due to the COVID-19 pandemic, there was lockdown and neither the family nor relatives were allowed to visit them. However, it is difficult for them to meet online *via* advanced technology like Zoom. Ultimately, it may harm their communication skills and social participation [21]. This also may decrease healthy life expectancy gradually in the long term.

2.2.2. Behind the Times

Mobile technology has become popular in contemporary society with the development of technological advancement. This is not convenient and easy for older people to use it, especially older adults with disabilities [8]. For example, the government released important information such as news related to COVID-19 and the Health Care Voucher Scheme and provided an electronic form for the Old Age Living Allowance application on the internet. Older adults may find it difficult to access information *via* the internet since they lack the knowledge to use the internet. They may feel disjointed with society and get upset since they cannot keep up with the trend. Therefore, this may pose a threat to their mental health, such as lowering their cognition and depression.

2.3. Demand Exceeds the Supply of Elderly Nursing Services

In the elderly nursing service market, the problem of exceeding demand becomes more intense. Hong Kong is facing a trend of increasing aging population. From 2016 to 2036, the number of older adults over 65 years old was expected to increase to around 121 million (14.5% of the total population). This leads to the increase in the demand for elderly nursing services. However, the labor force for older adults' service is facing a shortage. Table **3** shows that the vacancy rate of ward attendants in 2017 was 15.8% relatively high [22]. Almost all aged homes cannot hire enough employees to take care of residents. This increases the workload of existing ward attendants.

Table 3. Staff establishment, staff strength, and vacancy rate of the posts concerned 31 July 2017.

Post (Applicable to subsidized elderly and rehabilitation service units)	Staff Establishment	Staff Strength	Vacancy Rate
Personal care worker (PCW)	7403.5	6073.9	18.0%
Home helper (HH)	1318.0	1070.5	18.8%
Ward attendant (WA)	1643.5	1384.4	15.8%

Source: HKSAR (2017)

Most accidents that happened in aged homes were mainly because of the labor shortage and the heavy workload of WA. For example, in 2015, one older adult in residential care homes for the elderly (RCHEs) went missing, and this was anecdotal evidence. From 2012 to 2015, the Licensing Office of Residential Care Homes for the Elderly (LORCHE) received the report that around 180 missing residents from RCHEs [22]. In recent years, the incident of distributing incorrect drugs to the residents also happened. For example, in 2020, an 84-year-old woman was given the wrong medication. She was semi-conscious after consuming those incorrectly given medicines [23]. Therefore, this issue should be resolved.

3. RECOMMENDATIONS

3.1. Existing Mobile Healthcare Technologies in Hong Kong

Currently, there are three mobile healthcare technologies being operated in Hong Kong, namely HaGo, Electronic Health Record Sharing System (eHealth), and Care-on-Call Service. HaGo and eHealth are operated by hospital authorities, while Care-on-Call Service is operated by Senior Citizen Home Safety Association (SCHSA). Table **4** presents the comparison between the proposed new mobile app and the existing mobile healthcare technologies. The new app overcomes the weaknesses of current mobile healthcare technologies, optimizes the existing healthcare system, reduces workload, and improves patient safety.

Table 4. Comparison between the proposed new mobile app and the existing mobile healthcare technologies in Hong Kong.

Items	Year of Establishment	Querying Medical Records	Providing Regular Health Information	Regular Notification of Drug Consumption	Exclusive Use of Senior Citizen Card	Broadcasting Services	Chat Function	VR Connection
The proposed new mobile app	N/A	✓	✓	✓	✓	✓	✓	✓
HaGo	2019	✓	✗	✗	✗	✗	✗	✗
eHealth	2016	✓	✗	✗	✗	✗	✗	✗
Care-on-Call Service	1997	✗	✓	✓	✗	✗	✓	✗

Source: System [24], HaGo [25].

Compared with the new app, HaGo, Care-on-Call Service, and eHealth cannot offer the function of exclusive use of senior citizen cards, broadcasting services, and VR connection. The exclusive use of senior citizen cards is crucial to the aged home as it can reduce the workload for the staff.

Care-on-Call Service cannot offer the function of querying medical records. The staff and the older adults can check medical records and history in the new app. Hence, the new app can avoid the situation of giving the wrong medicine to older adults. Lacking this function, the staff fails to obtain any medical information about older adults using the care-on-call service.

HaGo and eHealth can only offer the function of querying medical records. Only the new app can support other functions like regular notification of drug consumption, providing regular health information, and chat functions. That means HaGo and eHealth cannot offer any entertainment and communication channels to older adults. Additionally, these two apps make it difficult to support the daily operation of an aged home because of lacking the function of regular notification of drug consumption.

In conclusion, the coverage of services provided is not as comprehensive as the new app. The new app takes care of both the older adults' mental and physical health conditions. Thus, the proposed new app offers a more comprehensive service than the three existing apps.

3.2. Design New Mobile App

To eliminate the older adults' mental barriers to smartphones, aged homes may develop a training and development team to promote the application and guide older adults. With the popularization of mobile devices, the proportion of older adults using smartphones has been very high. Application developers need to identify the critical issues faced by older adults when developing applications. When using mobile devices, older adults may experience technical anxiety and face some challenges due to complex user interfaces, lack of support systems, and visual issues [26]. Therefore, the three simple elements should be followed in the design, including giving a convenient user interface, avoiding complicated functions and irrelevant content, and providing a user guide.

In a convenient user interface, all aspects of human body function and vision will gradually degenerate with age. Older adults have poor eyesight and can be very troubled when they see small text. Thus, the new mobile phone application's default font size and pattern size should be the largest because some older adults do not know how to change the size. If the fonts and patterns are too small at first, they will be challenging to use. The color perception of older adults will also become worse. So, the color of the text should be brighter. This can form a strong contrast and make it easier for older adults to recognize what each design represents [27].

Due to less complicated functions and less irrelevant content, the simple design of mobile apps can attract older adults. These apps avoid slide-out menus because older adults need clear instructions [28]. They list all the functions on one main screen and provide two options "Return" and "Next Step". The button lets older adults know how to return to the main screen and proceed to the next step. In addition, gestures should be kept as simple as possible, such as simple taps and swipes. Avoid using complex gestures, for example, scrolling up to access the previous page [29].

Provide a user guide when older adults encounter problems with using mobile apps. Older adults will have a poor experience if they do not get help. It must set up 'a description button' to explain how to use all functions. If older adults want to use this function, what steps should be taken? For example, if older adults are going to use a medical service, specify in the 'Instructions' which button to press first and what to press after entering the screen to use this service. This makes them understand how to use the app [30].

3.2.1. Mobile App Functionalities

Functionality is also important for designing mobile applications [31]. It is preferred that every aged home installs devices that can be connected to the app and responsible for collecting health data of older adults for daily monitoring. So, staff may effectively manage the residents' condition in the aged home [32]. This study proposes and summarizes the innovative functions of the new mobile app in Table **5**.

Table 5. Functions of the new mobile app.

Functions	Rationale	Benefits
Querying medical records	Most older adults forget what medicine they need to take. They also do not know which illness they suffer from.	Older adults can record their medical records in this app. Nursing homes can more conveniently use the data collected by the system to provide corresponding care for every older adult. Allow older adults and nursing homes to view older adults' medical history, time of diagnosis, recurrence, and disease at any time.
Providing regular health information	Remind older adults to do moderate exercise and eat healthily, or give information on common diseases like heart disease, diabetes, or osteoporosis. This encourages older adults to prevent or delay diseases and avoid getting hurt during exercise.	Suggest some simple stretching training demonstration videos for older adults. They can follow the videos to carry out appropriate activities. For example, at 7 o'clock every day, aged homes send out messages uniformly to remind older adults to do an exercise taught by the app.
Regular notification of drug consumption	The physical function of older adults will deteriorate and have a high possibility of requiring medication. Older adults can first record times to take medicine on the app. Nursing caregivers can remind older adults. Since there are too many older adults in an aged home, the staff may forget to help them take medicine. This app can help to make the operation more fluent.	Older adults will not forget to take medicine. Nursing caregivers can remind them at once to save time for other tasks.

(Table 5) cont.....

Functions	Rationale	Benefits
Exclusive use of Senior Citizen Card	Older adults have a senior citizen card but sometimes do not understand how to use them. In addition, older adults may forget to bring a card. So, they cannot use the card to get a discount.	Older adults can learn the purpose of the senior citizen card through the app and enjoy preferential products and services under the program.
Broadcasting services	Older adults who are no longer attending community activities or visiting friends due to immobility. In this sense, they spend more time on broadcasting services.	Older adults can listen to the radio through the app. The app also provides text news headlines.
Chat function	Set up a platform to give older adults a place to relieve boredom. Some cannot find someone to talk to.	Older adults can use this service in the app to find a social worker and chat with them. The matched social worker may act as their 'Tree Hole'. Thus, the workload of nursing caregivers could be reduced. This idea is similar to 'The Samaritan Befrienders Hong Kong'.
VR connection	Older adults lack cognitive sentiments and reactions because of immobility.	Older adults can connect to the VR system through the app and enjoy entertainment activities by themselves. The staff can spend less time communicating/playing with them. Thus, the workload can be reduced.

Source: Grua *et al.* [31], Arkkukangas *et al.* [32], Lau and Chan [2]

3.2.2. VR Connection with Mobile Technology

It is better to use VR technology to provide more entertainment to older adults to promote a healthy lifestyle, reduce their social isolation, and maintain healthy psychology [2]. VR technology is a distinctive subset of mobile technology rising as a research discipline [33]. The following sub-section elaborates on the main functions of VR technology.

3.2.2.1. VR Technologies

The main functions of VR technologies include immersive VR experience, training programs, and linking with the mobile app.

• Immersive VR experience:

Older adults explore a VR headset to visit travel sites, making them feel like they are out of the door to ease their anxiety and loneliness [34]. Japanese Video Production Company Omoieizo has launched a 360° virtual reality experience service specifically designed for older adults with disabilities using a 3D VR camera to capture the Japanese scenery [35]. The immersive VR technology helps to improve the participants' motivation for rehabilitation and quality of life by supplementing their physical handicaps with technology. Since physical abilities decline in old age, going out becomes difficult for older adults. VR can help with daily healing and make them feel calmer to increase their social interactions through social participation and extend healthy life expectancy.

• Training program:

The program kits are suggested to provide a close-to-reality training environment using VR technologies for medical practitioners and patients. VR training allows older adults to break through their physical and environmental constraints [36]. For example, the Tung Wah Group of Hospitals developed a set of kits under the 'VRehab Generation' project, which was promoted in the aged home. It provides training services that include physical training, cognitive training, community living skills training, and relaxation. Older adults can participate in rehabilitation training regarding their progress purposefully and continuously in an enjoyable way. The study was observed by Dr. CHAU Pui Hing, Patsy. He found that participants of the 'VRehab Generation' improved their upper-limb dexterity and cognitive function. Although the project already ended on 31 March 2021, the success of the activity brings convenience to future planning.

• Links with the mobile app:

Older adults can enjoy entertainment and search the information online to increase their linkage with society through the mobile app mentioned above. VR technologies can link with the mobile app [33]. The researchers at Cambridge University implemented a navigation test using virtual reality to detect patients with early Alzheimer's (*i.e.*, the common disease that older adults have) and observed that it is more reliable than a traditional cognitive assessment. 'The Wayback' project can trigger precious memories and stimulate conversations in older adults to battle the effects of dementia and improve communication with families or care takers [37, 38].

3.2.3. Smartwatch for Nursing Homes

Many accidents happen because of the high workload of staff in nursing homes. However, it is impossible to increase the number of labor immediately. Therefore, it is necessary to use the function of the smartwatch to assist the labor. In this way, the efficiency of working can be enhanced, and human errors can be minimized.

3.2.3.1. Smartwatch Functions

Smartwatch for nursing homes is made up of a medical rubber, a natural and non-toxic material. It has a built-in lithium battery that has an endurance of up to 10 days. A PMOLED screen provides low power consumption and sunlight-readable solutions without harm to your vision. 128x128 resolution ensures accurate data display and easy operation for older adults [39]. Adopting the positioning technology based on GPS, GSM, Internet of Things (IoT), Wi-Fi networks, and a gravity sensor provides accurate real-time positioning, making it easy to position older adults at any time. Once older adults press the relevant button to call in an emergency, nursing aid can identify the situation and position of older adults immediately. The smartwatch has a waterproof design and safety buckle, specially designed for severely mentally retarded older adults. It can also display date, time, and contact phone numbers simultaneously. This is optimal for mildly, moderately, or severely mentally retarded older adults [40].

3.2.3.2. Features and Advantages

Three features are managed through the mobile app of nursing aids and smartwatches for older adults, which are intended to reduce the problems caused by manpower shortages through an intelligent operation.

• Record physical condition:

The smartwatch for nursing homes can keep track of the physical condition of older adults for the whole day. It monitors their heart rate and measures the oxygen saturation of the blood. Once the heart rate exceeds the safety limit for a certain period, the device will send a message to nursing aids to indicate that older adults are in danger or under pressure. It also can monitor other health data of older adults without manual operation, such as monitoring the blood sugar of patients with diabetes, blood pressure of patients with hypertension, and uric acid of common patients. Older adults can also know their health status anywhere at any time [34, 41]

• Real-time dynamic accurate positioning:

Real-time dynamic accurate positioning is one of the functions of a smartwatch for nursing homes. This function supports a synchronous display of mobile phone position and app navigation. With Google positioning technology, the device can perform real-time dynamic positioning of older adults [42]. This is convenient for nursing aids to accurately locate older adults in real-time, know their current situation, and search for the movement scope through a one-click operation [43].

The watch supports defining a safe zone and sends an alarm to family members or nursing aid once the elderly are out of the safe zone.

• Emergency call:

Once older adults press and hold the SOS button in an emergency case, the app will send an alarm at maximum volume immediately and display the detailed data of the position on the app where the SOS signal was sent out. Meanwhile, the mobile phone will receive an SOS message sent by the watch to ensure an immediate, timely response to any emergency and guarantee the safety of older adults through an emergency call and real-time positioning functions [44]. The heart rate monitoring system can send an alarm to nursing aids once older adults are in poor physical condition. For example, the Apple watch can automatically monitor whether users are violently knocked down or fallen. Once monitoring is completed, the device will prompt users to check if they are in good condition. If users fail to respond within one minute, the device will automatically contact the emergency service. The device is specially designed for patients with Parkinson's disease at risk of falling or for older adults. Nursing aids must conduct real-time dynamic monitoring of such people to reduce the risk of falling [40].

3.2.4. Implementation

This section identifies the possible solutions for implementing the proposed mobile integrated system. To develop the proposed VR training program and monitoring system, the system is divided into user and management platforms. In the management platforms, the system is connected to the IoT devices such as smartwatches and other mobile devices. The management platforms receive the data directly from the cloud server in which the patient's big data are stored in the cloud platform. In contrast, the data analytics are transmitted to the management platform through the queries of the API.

The management platform provides a dashboard that presents the patient's training record systematically. To receive data from the user's side, the VR training program is developed using the game engine converted into the mobile application format for deployment. When patients participate in the VR training, the mobile phone receives necessary data through the sensors in the device. The data are uploaded to the cloud platform for analysis to provide essential information about the management for review and diagnosis [45 - 47].

It is suggested to use LowCode/NoCode platforms to develop mobile apps. It is feasible to use the graphical interface to configure apps in a short period without/with minimal code to build the MVP. During the testing phase, it would be easier to make changes to the feedback from the actual users without reviewing or changing the codes [36]. We will rely on Outsystems [48] to support IOS and Android. Such a system is the pioneer in the market, and lots of professional developers and citizen developers are using it every day.

The following points discuss implementing mobile technology for older adults in a sustainable way.

• Seek government financial assistance to prepare research and development funds for investment, such as enhanced tax deductions for R&D expenditures, enterprise support schemes, and innovation and technology funds [38]. Developers can make sure apps have enough budget to design and develop apps [49]. Follow-up of miscellaneous expenses, listing costs, and operating costs are also necessary to have a sufficient budget [50, 51].

• Cooperate with firms specializing in the development of apps, utilizing the other party's advanced technical equipment and professional knowledge to speed up the time to market products [52]. The Innovation and Technology Commission [53] established the Research Talent Hub, allowing us to recruit research talents to conduct research, invention, development, and innovation.

• Recruit professional and technical personnel to sustain the program. It is necessary to update the information regularly to ensure the smooth operation of the function. Also, the internal functions and contents of apps can be modified after launching [54].

• Design promotional campaigns for different nursing homes and community centers. It may publicize how the app is used and what it does, such as arranging volunteers to teach at the center.

• Maintain close collaboration with relevant government departments. The health and welfare sectors may regularly update information on matters needing attention for older adults living alone at home, elderly welfare, and basic health knowledge. Hospitals may update personal medical records, such as drug sensitivity and injection records, date of follow-up visits, and diagnosis.

• Older adults and staff may not know how to use the app. Therefore, we may cooperate with some projects to help them learn how to use technological devices. One of the projects is the LU Jockey Club Gerontechnology and Smart Ageing Project, offering gerontechnology practitioner training courses to older adults and their caregivers. The Guardians of the Silver Age also has a new eldercare talent training program and established a comprehensive training and employment system. Older adults can learn technical skills and innovative concepts through this system, including gerontechnology and the re-enablement care model [55].

CONCLUSION

This study contributes to academic and industrial practice. This study analyzed mobile technologies' design and implications for the elderly. Suggestions and recommendations were made to solve the issues faced by aged homes. As a rising trend of using smartphones, older adults may enjoy the benefit of mobile technology. Mobile technology might be fully implemented in health and other industries in the long term. People will be made familiar with the usage of mobile technology. The manpower shortage will not be a problem anymore because this technology saves time and human efforts. This will also make it easier for staff to provide better support to older adults and monitor their health condition.

This study is critical as the basic idea for developing technologies was to support health staff in better servicing older adults and monitoring their symptoms. The health sector can use the findings to improve services for other people with different illnesses. This may reduce future burden on healthcare systems and provide recommendations for emergency care.

Mobile technology is one of the assistive technologies. To this end, this study comprehensively reviews the existing mobile healthcare technologies. Accordingly, the study highlights how design principles and device characteristics of mobile technology decrease the gap between older adults' demand and their needs. The study also investigates how older adults are considered during the design process of the mobile app. Additionally, the study explores how to design and implement mobile technology to foster older adults in smart cities.

Aged homes are now eager to develop mobile technologies with academic institutions or consultancy firms. Through this study, they may get an idea to produce new innovative mobile technology products. Most aged homes face financial constraints and human resource limitations. With sufficient research funding support, aged homes can deliver excellent service performance for older adults *via* the application of mobile technology.

However, this study has some limitations that may need to be overcome in future research. First, the study provided a preliminary study relevant to the design and implementation of mobile technology for older adults but did not consider the perspectives and other research approaches. Also, the viewpoints of health professionals, policymakers, industry practitioners, mobile phone operators, and app builders are overlooked. Future research should develop a theoretical framework and validate it using a large-scale questionnaire survey from these perspectives. Future research may also conduct in-depth interviews with health professionals, policymakers, industry practitioners, mobile phone operators, and app developers. Also, this study focused only on Hong Kong, which may encounter weaknesses in invalidity, generalizability, and reliability. To generalize the study, future research should consider other Asian countries, such as Taiwan, Japan, South Korea, and China. Moreover, the study lacks a new concept to develop interdisciplinary studies between health and engineering. The research areas or concepts like the adoption of technology in long-term care, blockchain in healthcare, machine learning in healthcare service delivery, and the use of mixed reality in healthcare should be considered in future studies.

REFERENCES

[1]   Yusof MFM, Romli N, Yusof MFM. Design for elderly friendly: Mobile phone application and design that suitable for elderly. Int J Comput Appl 2014; 95.

[2]   Lau Y-Y, Chan I. The implications of virtual reality (VR) for the aged. cases on virtual reality modeling in healthcare.Cases on Virtual Reality Modeling in Healthcare. IGI Global 2022.
[http://dx.doi.org/10.4018/978-1-7998-8790-4.ch003]

[3]   Raman J. Mobile technology in nursing education: Where do we go from here? A review of the literature. Nurse Educ Today 2015; 35(5): 663-72.
[http://dx.doi.org/10.1016/j.nedt.2015.01.018] [PMID: 25665926]

[4]   Su KW, Liu CL. A mobile nursing information system based on human-computer interaction design for improving quality of nursing. J Med Syst 2012; 36(3): 1139-53.
[http://dx.doi.org/10.1007/s10916-010-9576-y] [PMID: 20827569]

[5]   Lau Y, Tang YM, Chau KY, Vyas L, Sandoval-Hernandez A, Wong S. COVID-19 crisis: exploring community of inquiry in online learning for sub-degree students. Front Psychol 2021; 12: 679197.
[http://dx.doi.org/10.3389/fpsyg.2021.679197] [PMID: 34366999]

[6]   Choo C, Kuek J, Burton A. Smartphone applications for mindfulness interventions with suicidality in Asian older adults: A literature review. Int J Environ Res Public Health 2018; 15(12): 2810.
[http://dx.doi.org/10.3390/ijerph15122810] [PMID: 30544738]

[7]   Lee KS, Eom JK, Lee J, Ko S. Analysis of the activity and travel patterns of the elderly using mobile phone-based hourly locational trajectory data: Case study of gangnam, korea. Sustainability 2021; 13(6): 3025.
[http://dx.doi.org/10.3390/su13063025]

[8]   Iancu I, Iancu B. Designing mobile technology for elderly. A theoretical overview. Technol Forecast Soc Change 2020; 155: 119977.
[http://dx.doi.org/10.1016/j.techfore.2020.119977]

[9]   Feist H, Parker K, Howard N, Hugo G. New technologies: Their potential role in linking rural older people to community. Int J Emerg Technol Soc 2010; 8: 68.

[10]   Damant J, Knapp M. What are the likely changes in society and technology which will impact upon the ability of older adults to maintain social (extra-familial) networks of support now, in 2025 and in 2040?. Jacqueline Damant and Martin Knapp Personal Social Services Research Unit London School of Economics and Political Science 2015.

[11]   Gomez-Hernandez M, Adrian SW, Ferre X, Villalba-Mora E. Implicit, explicit, and structural barriers and facilitators for information and communication technology access in older adults. Front Psychol 2022; 13: 874025.
[http://dx.doi.org/10.3389/fpsyg.2022.874025] [PMID: 35719540]

[12]   Kwak C, Kim S, You S, Han W. Development of the hearing rehabilitation for older adults (HeRO) healthcare mobile application and its likely utility for elderly users. Int J Environ Res Public Health 2020; 17(11): 3998.
[http://dx.doi.org/10.3390/ijerph17113998] [PMID: 32512885]

[13]   Matthew-Maich N, Harris L, Ploeg J, *et al.* Designing, implementing, and evaluating mobile health technologies for managing chronic conditions in older adults: A scoping review. JMIR Mhealth Uhealth 2016; 4(2): e29.
[http://dx.doi.org/10.2196/mhealth.5127] [PMID: 27282195]

[14]   Wong K, Yeung M. Population ageing trend of Hong Kong. Population 2019; 18: 64.

[15]   Department CAS. Hong Kong Census and Statisitcs. 2021. Available from: https://www.censtatd.gov.hk/en/ (accessed 25 May 2022).

[16]   Vaportzis E, Giatsi Clausen M, Gow AJ. Older adults perceptions of technology and barriers to interacting with tablet computers: A focus group study. Front Psychol 2017; 8: 1687.
[http://dx.doi.org/10.3389/fpsyg.2017.01687] [PMID: 29071004]

[17]   Backes C, Moyano C, Rimaud C, Bienvenu C, Schneider MP. Digital medication adherence support: Could healthcare providers recommend mobile health apps? Frontiers in Medical Technology 2021; 2: 616242.
[http://dx.doi.org/10.3389/fmedt.2020.616242] [PMID: 35047896]

[18]   Knickman JR, Snell EK. The 2030 problem: Caring for aging baby boomers. Health Serv Res 2002; 37(4): 849-84.
[http://dx.doi.org/10.1034/j.1600-0560.2002.56.x] [PMID: 12236388]

[19]   Chakraborty D. Elements impacting the utilization expectation of various health-care apps in India: A study conducted on smartphone users. Foresight 2020; 22(3): 385-400.
[http://dx.doi.org/10.1108/FS-11-2019-0098]

[20]   Isabet B, Pino M, Lewis M, Benveniste S, Rigaud AS. Social telepresence robots: A narrative review of experiments involving older adults before and during the COVID-19 pandemic. Int J Environ Res Public Health 2021; 18(7): 3597.
[http://dx.doi.org/10.3390/ijerph18073597] [PMID: 33808457]

[21]   Againg NIO. Social isolation, loneliness in older people pose health risks. 2019. Available from: https://www.nia.nih.gov/news/social-isolation-loneliness-older-people-pose-health-risks (accessed 31 January 2022).

[22]   HKSAR. Manpower shortage in elderly service sector: The Government of Hong Kong Special Administrative Region. 2017. Available from: https://www.info.gov.hk/gia/general/201711/29/P2017112900367.htm?fontSize=1 (Accessed 31 January 2022).

[23]   Maisy M, Wang W. Rodent horror at home for the elderly 2020. Available from: https://www.thestandard.com.hk/section-news/section/4/223120/Rodent-horr-r-at-home-for-the-elderly (Accessed 31 January 2022).

[24]   System EHRS. 2022. Available from: https://www.ehealth.gov.hk/en/index.html (accessed 15 February 2022).

[25]   Hago.. 2022. Available from: https://www2.ha.org.hk/hago/about-ha-go/ha-go/what-is-ha-go (accessed 15 February 2022).

[26]   Singh T. 7 Problems Elderly face when using smartphones. 2019. Available from: https://otakuwizard.com/problems-elderly-face-when-using-smartphones/ (accessed 7 October 2021).

[27]   Alsswey A, Al-Samarraie H. Elderly users' acceptance of mHealth user interface (UI) design-based culture: The moderator role of age. J Multimodal User Interfaces 2020; 14(1): 49-59.
[http://dx.doi.org/10.1007/s12193-019-00307-w]

[28]   Compañó R. Converging applications for active ageing policy. Foresight 2006.

[29]   Morey SA, Stuck RE, Chong AW, Barg-Walkow LH, Mitzner TL, Rogers WA. Mobile health apps: Improving usability for older adult users. Ergon Des 2019; 27(4): 4-13.
[http://dx.doi.org/10.1177/1064804619840731]

[30] Yang HL, Lin SL. The reasons why elderly mobile users adopt ubiquitous mobile social service. Comput Human Behav 2019; 93: 62-75.
[http://dx.doi.org/10.1016/j.chb.2018.12.005]

[31] Grua EM, De Sanctis M, Malavolta I, Hoogendoorn M, Lago P. An evaluation of the effectiveness of personalization and self-adaptation for e-Health apps. Inf Softw Technol 2022; 146: 106841.
[http://dx.doi.org/10.1016/j.infsof.2022.106841]

[32] Arkkukangas M, Cederbom S, Tonkonogi M, Umb Carlsson Õ. Older adults' experiences with mHealth for fall prevention exercise: usability and promotion of behavior change strategies. Physiother Theory Pract 2021; 37(12): 1346-52.
[http://dx.doi.org/10.1080/09593985.2020.1712753] [PMID: 31910707]

[33] Liao T. Future directions for mobile augmented reality research: Understanding relationships between augmented reality users, nonusers, content, devices, and industry. Mob Media Commun 2019; 7(1): 131-49.
[http://dx.doi.org/10.1177/2050157918792438]

[34] Laua Y-Y, Tangb YM, Chauc KY, Huib HY. Pilot study of heartbeat sensors for data streaming in virtual reality (VR) training. Int J Innov Creat Chang 2021; 15: 30-41.

[35] Chen J. A dedicated 360 VR service for the dying? Go back to your hometown in a second and see the scenery of your childhood to make your dream come true. 2019. Available from: https://www.hk01.com/%E6%95%B8%E7%A2%BC%E7%94%9F%E6%B4%BB/364124/%E8%87%A8%E7%B5%82%E4%BA%BA%E5%A3%AB%E5%B0%88%E7%94%A8-360-vr-%E6%9C%8D%E5%8B%99-%E4%B8%80%E7%A7%92%E5%9B%9E%E5%88%B0%E6%95%85%E9%84%89-%E5%86%8D%E7%9C%8B%E5%85%92%E6%99%82%E6%99%AF%E8%89%B2%E5%9C%93%E5%A4%A2 accessed 15 February 2022).

[36] Fong KNK, Tang YM, Sie K, Yu AKH, Lo CCW, Ma YWT. Task-specific virtual reality training on hemiparetic upper extremity in patients with stroke. Virtual Real 2022; 26(2): 453-64.
[http://dx.doi.org/10.1007/s10055-021-00583-6]

[37] Roznovsky A. 10 uses of virtual reality in medicine. 2020. Available from: https://light-it.net/blog/virtual-reality-in-medicine/

[38] Saygitov R T. Health-related R&D priorities until 2030: Russian experience. Foresight 2017; 19(5): 501-10.
[http://dx.doi.org/10.1108/FS-06-2016-0022]

[39] Ali H, Li H. Evaluating a smartwatch notification system in a simulated nursing home. Int J Older People Nurs 2019; 14(3): e12241.
[http://dx.doi.org/10.1111/opn.12241] [PMID: 31099184]

[40] Flores-Martin D, Rojo J, Moguel E, Berrocal J, Murillo JM. Smart nursing homes: Self-management architecture based on iot and machine learning for rural areas. Wirel Commun Mob Comput 2021; 2021: 1-15.
[http://dx.doi.org/10.1155/2021/8874988]

[41] Stavropoulos TG, Papastergiou A, Mpaltadoros L, Nikolopoulos S, Kompatsiaris I. IoT wearable sensors and devices in elderly care: A literature review. Sensors 2020; 20(10): 2826.
[http://dx.doi.org/10.3390/s20102826] [PMID: 32429331]

[42] Wang Z, Yang Z, Dong T. A review of wearable technologies for elderly care that can accurately track indoor position, recognize physical activities and monitor vital signs in real time. Sensors 2017; 17(2): 341.
[http://dx.doi.org/10.3390/s17020341] [PMID: 28208620]

[43] Reinhardt T. Using Global Localization to Improve Navigation. 2019. Available from: https://ai.googleblog.com/2019/02/using-global-localization-to-improve.html (Accessed 28 February 2022).

[44] King CE, Sarrafzadeh M. A survey of smartwatches in remote health monitoring. J Healthc Inform Res 2018; 2(1-2): 1-24.
[http://dx.doi.org/10.1007/s41666-017-0012-7] [PMID: 30035250]

[45] Tang YM, Yu KM. Development and evaluation of a mobile platform for teaching mathematics of CAD subjects. Comput Aided Des Appl 2018; 15(2): 164-9.
[http://dx.doi.org/10.1080/16864360.2017.1375665]

[46] Tang YM, Chau KY, Kwok APK, Zhu T, Ma X. A systematic review of immersive technology applications for medical practice and education-trends, application areas, recipients, teaching contents, evaluation methods, and performance. Educ Res Rev 2021; 100429.

[47] Tang YM, Chau KY, Xu D, Liu X. Consumer perceptions to support IoT based smart parcel locker logistics in China. J Retailing Consum Serv 2021; 62: 102659.
[http://dx.doi.org/10.1016/j.jretconser.2021.102659]

[48] Outsystems. 2022. Available from: http://www.outsystems.com (accessed 15 May 20220).

[49] Butter M, Hoogendoorn J. Foresight versus FP7: Comparing innovations in healthcare. Foresight 2008; 10(6): 39-61.
[http://dx.doi.org/10.1108/14636680810918577]

[50] Fund IAT. 2022. Available from: https://www.itf.gov.hk/en/home/index.html (accessed 15 May 2022).

[51] Investhk. Enhanced tax deduction for R&D expenditures. 2022. Available from: https://www.investhk.gov.hk/en/resource-centre/enhanced-tax-deduction-rd-expenditures.html (Accessed 15 May 2022).

[52] Kaplan AM. If you love something, let it go mobile: Mobile marketing and mobile social media 4x4. Bus Horiz 2012; 55(2): 129-39.
[http://dx.doi.org/10.1016/j.bushor.2011.10.009]

[53] Commission IAT. 2022. Available from: https://www.itc.gov.hk/en/index.html (accessed 16 May 2022).

[54] Anderson K, Burford O, Emmerton L. Mobile health apps to facilitate self-care: A qualitative study of user experiences. PLoS One 2016; 11(5): e0156164.
[http://dx.doi.org/10.1371/journal.pone.0156164] [PMID: 27214203]

[55] Kong GH. 2022. Available from: https://en.hongkong.generation.org/eldercare/?gclid=EAIaIQobChMIloKyz6vq9gIV1quWCh3oNAY MEAAYASAAEgKNPfD_BwE (Accessed 16 May 2022).

Virtual Reality, Artificial Intelligence, 2023, 125-140

The Application of Macro Business Simulation on Healthcare Product: Hand Sanitizer

Abstract: This book chapter mainly discusses how Macro Business Simulation applies to healthcare products. Due to the COVID-19 pandemic, hand sanitizer is a necessity to minimize the spread of the COVID-19 virus to the public. To the best of the authors' knowledge, the International Association of Business Management Simulation launched macro business simulations over the past few years across academic institutions, firms, and training bodies. Macro business simulation games become emerging educational tools due to the growth of online learning pedagogy and the emergence of innovative educational concepts. This book chapter mainly identifies the key elements of macro business simulation, expected students' learning outcomes, and the key structures of macro business simulation. Hand sanitizer is also used as an illustrative example to investigate how healthcare products integrate into the macro business simulation platform.

Keywords: Macro business simulation, Healthcare products, Hand sanitizer, International Association of Business Management Simulation.

1. INTRODUCTION

1.1. What Do Students Learn About?

● Budgeting –Why do the students need to allocate appropriate numbers to their budget plans by making sound decisions? The educators may conduct a comparison of their accounting with their budgeting to understand their deviations.

● Decision Making – The main role of an executive is to make wise decisions. The students may make numerous decisions, for instance, whether to buy or rent their production lines.

● Product Calculations – What volume of products should students produce, given the costs and the market demand? What prices should they accept when selling in the market?

Yui-yip Lau, Tang Yuk Ming & Leung Wai Keung Alan

● Investment Analysis – Would we allocate the research funding to decrease production costs? Would we finance the new factory? Which new product line do we provide capital for?

● Risk Assessment – If all goes smoothly, can we still fulfill the commitments in our investments?

● Dividend Strategy – How will paying dividends affect how the market values your company?

● Cash flow management – The students will be required to closely monitor their cash flow. They may apply for loans or retain profits. Otherwise, they will bear expensive credit in case of using up money.

● Accounting – The simulation game can systematically establish cash flow statements, balance sheets, and profit and loss statements. Alternatively, you may let the students take the bookkeeping exercises themselves.

● Strategy – link the points between various academic disciplines including finance, operations, strategy, operations, and accounting. In what way are the finances of a cost leader strategy compared to a skimming-the-market strategy?

2. BASIC GAME SCENARIO

Macro Business Simulation (MBS) is a single product, one-to-four markets business game. Product demand is seasonal and affected by individual market prices, product image and quality, and other economic factors. Each round of the game can be considered a quarter of the calendar time.

MBS has four models of the game with a number of decisions see Table **1**. The game can accommodate up to 20 groups of players, up to 6 players with different management roles in a group. The CEO is a "super player" and can take on any extra roles if needed. All players save their decisions temporarily and only the CEO can submit the decisions for the company. Once decisions are submitted, no change will be allowed.

Model 1 and 2 games are suitable for practice purposes because they have only one market and fewer decisions. These games will introduce all players to familiarize the structure of the game, available reports and analysis, and decision-making logic.

Table 1. Level of decision making.

Model	Raw Materials Purchasing	Production Qty Allocation	Retail (Prices and Markets)	Marketing Expenses	Equipment I Maintenance	R&D Expenses	Dividend	Loan	Number of Decisions
1	√	√	√	√	-	-	-	-	4
2	√	√	√	√	√	√	√	√	-	8
3	√	√	√√√√	√√√√	√	√	√	√	-	14
4	√	√√√√	√√√√	√√√√	√	√	√	√	√	18
-	Purchasing Manager	Production Manager	Sales Manager	Planning Manager	Production Manager	Planning Manager	Financial Manager	Financial Manager	-

Model 3 and 4 games extend the business scenarios with four individual markets with different pricing and marketing investment decisions. The production mode also allows up to three shifts a day to expand the capacity needed to meet the potential demand [1].

3. MANAGEMENT DASHBOARD

Once you log in to the system, the management dashboard will be displayed with key performance indicators (KPIs) and related information (Fig. **1**).

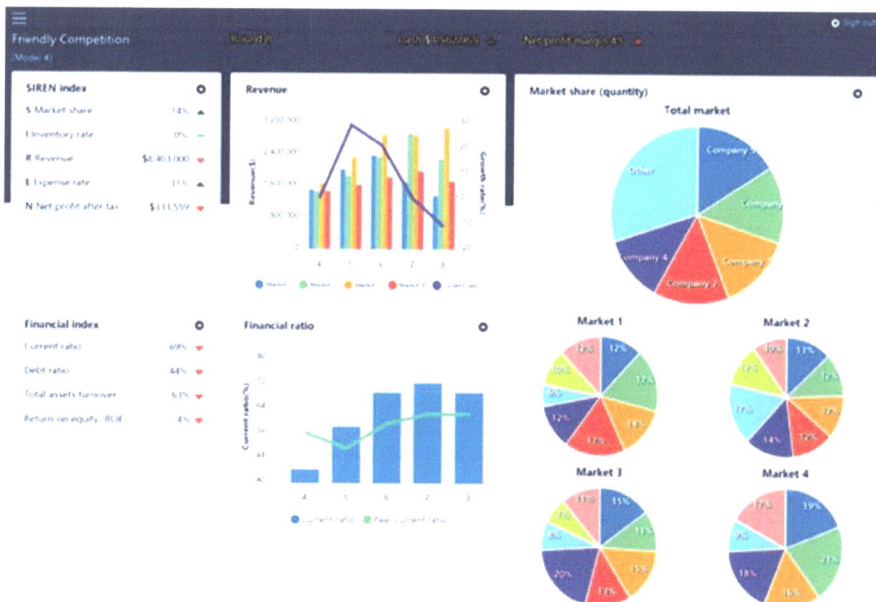

Fig. (1). Management dashboard.

3.1. SIREN Index

● Market share = Total sales of a company / Total sales of all participating companies.

● Inventory rate = Finished goods Inventory / Sales volume.

● Revenue = Total sales revenue of a company in all markets.

● Expense ratio = Total operating expense / Total sales revenue where Total operating expense = Marketing expense + Admin expense (in the Income statement).

● Net profit = Total revenue – Cost of goods sold – Total operating expense (incl. Depreciation) – Interest – Tax.

3.2. Financial Index

● Current ratio = Current assets / Current liabilities where Current liabilities are the same as total liabilities as there is no long-term debt in MBS games.

● Debt ratio = Total liabilities / Total assets.

● Total asset turnover = Total sales revenue / Total assets.

● ROE = Net profit / Owner's equity where Net profit = Earnings after interest and tax.

● Net profit margin = Net profit / Total sales revenue.

4. BASIC GAME SETTINGS

You should review carefully key business and economic conditions in **Business Overview > Environment** before making any decisions. These game settings are determined by your instructor and will change when starting a new game (Fig. **2**).

The market share deferred effect consists of three levels: high, moderate, and low [1].

Price elasticity indicates the effect of price competition in individual markets, as well as includes three main levels: low, moderate, and high.

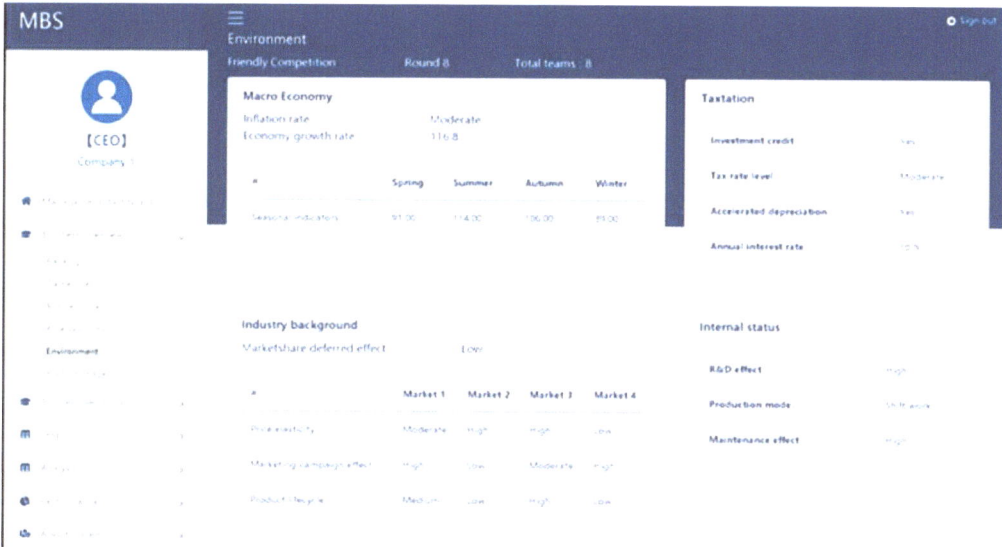

Fig. (2). Basic game settings.

Marketing campaign impact indicates the promotion effect of marketing expense in individual markets along with three key levels, namely, low, moderate, and high. Marketing investment will maintain about a 30% impact after the first round. The actual impact is also subject to other competitors' decisions.

The market growth rate is the so-called product lifecycle that determines individual markets. In general, it is divided into three main levels such as low growth, moderate growth, and high growth. In the beginning, the cycle begins with 0. The aggregate value progressively improves with the evolution of the market. Then, the market comes to mature along with the whole possibility of demand emerging as saturated when the value attained in 2. The sales volume diminishes when the product life cycle is at the decline stage.

The R&D effect serves to influence product quality (and subsequently potential demand) and consists of three levels: high, moderate, and low. It also affects production efficiency (please refer to the Material conversion factor in the Income statement). R&D investment will maintain about a 60% impact after the round. The actual impact is also subject to other competitors' decisions.

Production mode relates to the production policy of the company.

• For Model 1 and 2 games, only one shift is allowed with at most 50% of overtime production capacity.

● For Model 3 and 4 games, the shift choices are automatically decided by the system in accordance with the production quantity needed for the round and the availability of raw materials (plus urgent purchases). The production capacity could be set at different discrete levels: 1 shift, 1.35 shifts (with overtime), 2 shifts, 2.5 shifts (with overtime), and 3 shifts.

The maintenance effect serves to influence product quality (and subsequently potential demand) and production efficiency (The material conversion factor) and pertains to three main levels of low, moderate, and high. Spending on maintenance can only create an impact during the round.

5. ECONOMIC STATUS REPORT

The Economy report (MBS > Status > Economy) provides you with information such as price index, economic growth rate, seasonal indicators, and the product lifecycle in each market. These indicators will affect the overall market to the same extent, except for the product lifecycle, which is market-dependent (Fig. **3**).

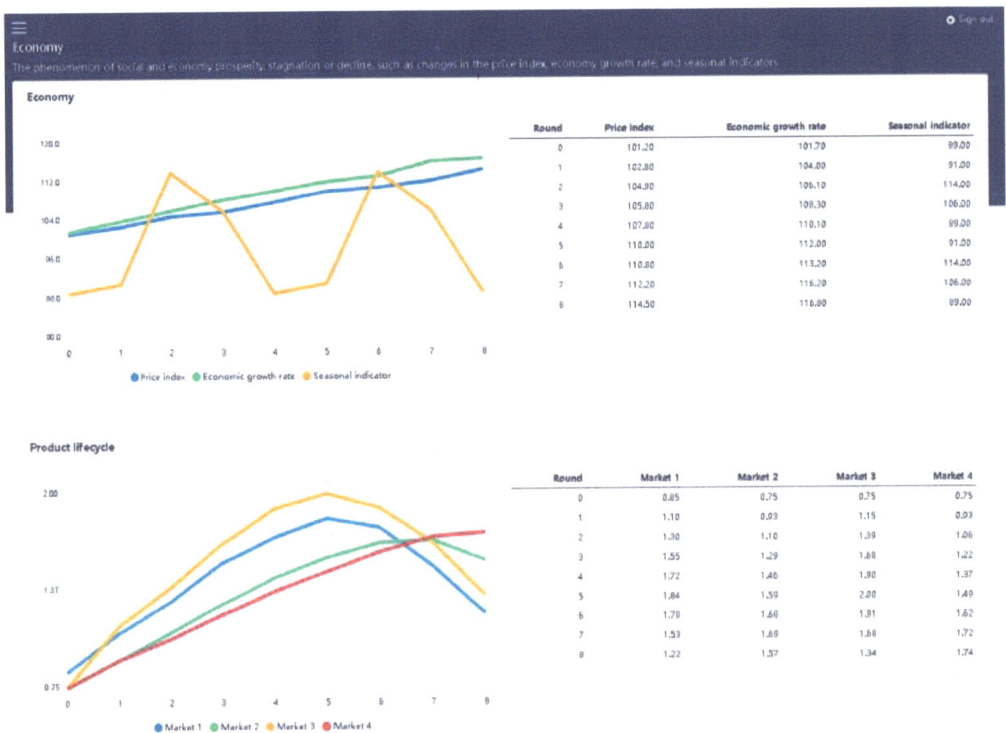

Round	Price index	Economic growth rate	Seasonal indicator
0	101.20	101.70	99.00
1	102.80	104.00	91.00
2	104.90	106.10	114.00
3	105.80	108.30	106.00
4	107.80	110.10	99.00
5	110.00	112.00	91.00
6	110.80	113.20	114.00
7	112.20	116.20	106.00
8	114.50	118.80	99.00

Round	Market 1	Market 2	Market 3	Market 4
0	0.85	0.75	0.75	0.75
1	1.10	0.93	1.15	0.93
2	1.30	1.10	1.39	1.06
3	1.55	1.29	1.68	1.22
4	1.72	1.46	1.90	1.37
5	1.84	1.59	2.00	1.49
6	1.78	1.68	1.91	1.62
7	1.53	1.69	1.68	1.72
8	1.22	1.57	1.34	1.74

Fig. (3). Economic status report.

The price index is a measurement of inflation, and it will affect your pricing strategies, and purchase cost of raw materials and equipment. There are four types of inflation you may encounter in the game: severe inflation, moderate inflation, mild inflation, and negative inflation (deflation). The price index often refers to the government-published consumer (or producer) price index.

The economic growth rate will affect the purchasing power and hence the potential demand. It is usually measured by GDP growth.

Seasonal indicators will affect the potential demand for your company's product. A seasonal indicator of 100 or more indicates stronger demand than normal and *vice versa*.

Product lifecycle refers to the market growth rate (which is also determined by how fast it undergoes product introduction to peak demand) and will affect the potential demand for your company's product in individual markets. The potential demand indicator at round 0 is 1 (default) and will become 2 at the peak with the potential demand doubles. Demand will decline steadily after the peak. The potential demand in each market may also vary depending on how each company sets its price and investment there.

● High: It takes about 5 rounds to reach the peak demand potential.

● Medium: It takes about 8 rounds to reach the peak demand potential.

● Low: It takes about 15 rounds to reach the peak demand potential.

6. BUSINESS STATUS REPORT

The Business status report (MBS > Status > Business status) provides you with a quick overview of your company's sales volume and production capacity. You can review the information at each round to have a better understanding of how to synchronize your potential demand with the next production capacity. Note that the next production capacity refers to one shift only, but you may use overtime or up to three shifts (for model 3 and 4 games) to meet the potential demand (Fig. 4).

Potential demand refers to the total amount of orders (product units) received by the company in the current round and is affected by the company's current and previous prices, marketing expense, R&D expense, market share in the previous round, deferred market potential in the previous round, economy, seasonal indices, and price fluctuations.

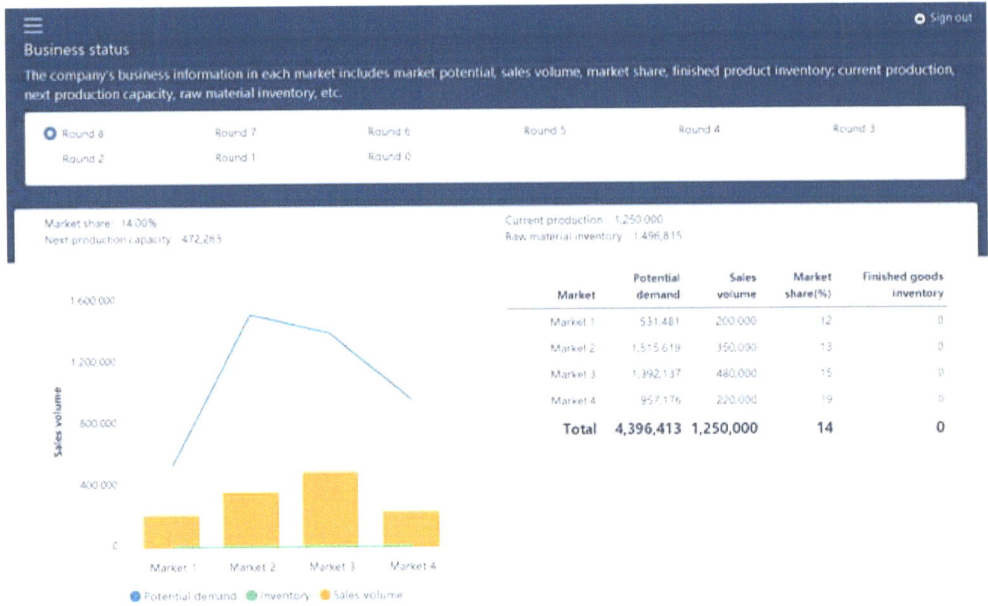

Fig. (4). Business status report.

Current production is the maximum production volume in the current round, limited by available raw materials or production capacity, whichever is smaller.

Finished goods inventory = Finished goods inventory from the previous round + current production quantity – Current sales quantity.

Market share (%) shows the company's own share in each of the markets.

Sales volume is the actual sales quantity of the company in the current round.

Next production capacity refers to the number of products that a single shift can produce without overtime.

Next production capacity = Current production capacity x (1 – Depreciation rate) + Current new equipment investment / 20 x Price index.

7. SALES/Production Analysis

The Sales/Production analysis (MBS > Analysis > Production/Logistics) provides you with information such as sales volume, production capacity, raw material inventory, and finished goods inventory (Fig. **5**).

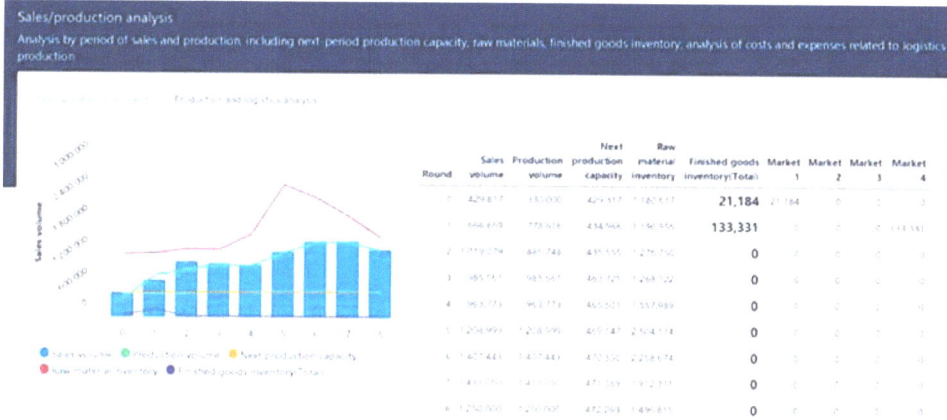

Fig. (5). Sales/production analysis.

Sales volume refers to the actual sales quantity of the company in the current round.

Production volume refers to the current production quantity and is limited by available raw materials or production capacity, whichever is smaller. That is, when the quantity of available raw materials (*i.e.*, inventory of previous round + material purchased in previous round + urgent purchase of material in current round) is insufficient or the production capacity is not enough to meet the production request/allocation, the current production volume = the maximum production volume, which can be less than the production request/allocation.

Next production capacity refers to the number of products that a single shift can produce without overtime work.

Next production capacity = Current production capacity x (1 – Depreciation rate) + Current new equipment investment / ($20 x Price index).

Example: Current round = 8, Current capacity = 471,390, Depreciation = 2.5%, Current equipment investment = $300,000, Price index = 1.145.

Next production capacity = 471,390 (1 – 2.5%) + $300,000 / ($20 x 1.145) = 459,605 + 13,100 = 472,705.

For reference: Business rules on equipment investment. For every $20 investment, the next period can gain production capacity increase by one unit. To avoid significant increases in business risks, investment should be no more than half of the equity of each period.

Raw material inventory refers to the number of raw materials at the end of the round.

Raw material inventory = Raw material inventory from the previous round + Purchase of raw materials in the previous round (so they will be available in the current round) + Urgent purchase of raw materials in the current round *(for Model 4 games only)* – Current consumption of raw materials.

Finished goods inventory (Total) refers to the total quantity of raw materials in all markets at the end of the round.

Finished goods inventory (Total) = Finished goods inventory from the previous round + Current production volume – Current sales volume.

8. DEMAND–SUPPLY COORDINATION DECISIONS OF INDIVIDUAL MARKETS

To synchronize supply and demand, you can use the sales and operations plan (SOP) as a tool. In MBS games, the following business rules will be applied:

- Potential demand = f (Price, Marketing, and R&D expenses).

- Production capacity = f (Equipment investment and Maintenance).

- Max available sales volume in each market = Production allocation + Finished goods inventory.

- Actual sales volume = Min (Potential demand, Max volume available for sales).

The following diagram Fig. (6) shows the decisions related to potential demand, production capacity, and production request/allocation. You enter these decision parameters in MBS > Business decisions > Make decisions.

Maximum volume available for sales = Production allocation + Finished goods inventory.

- If Potential demand ≤ Max available, Actual sales volume = Potential demand. Any leftover stock will be carried over to the next round as the beginning inventory of finished goods.

- If Potential demand > Max is available, Actual sales volume = Maximum volume available for sales, and 70% of unsatisfied demand will be shared by other companies (to increase their Potential demand in the current round) and the remaining 30% will become lost sales for the company. The Potential demand for the current round shown on the business status report will be adjusted downward to exclude the lost sales quantity, *i.e.*, Revised potential demand = Original potential demand x 0.7.

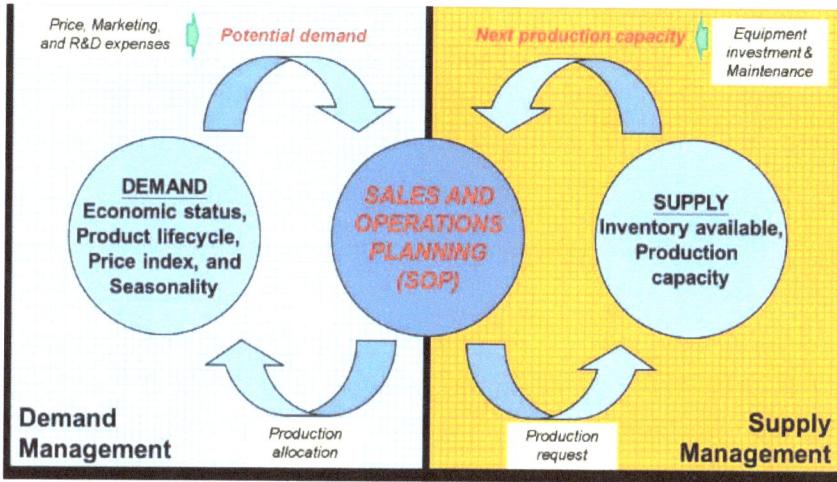

Fig. (6). Supply and demand synchronization.

Sales volume of individual market = Sales volume x Individual potential demand / Aggregate potential demand.

Production allocation = Current production capacity = Previous production capacity x 0.975 + Previous equipment investment / (20 x T+3's price index).

• If there are sufficient raw materials and production capacity, Actual production = Production request or allocation.

• If there are insufficient raw materials or insufficient production capacity, Actual production = Min (Current production capacity of finished goods, Available raw materials).

• Raw materials can, if inadequate, be supplemented by urgent procurement *(available only for the Model 4 game)*, and current production capacity is the primary factor restricting actual production.

• In the event of insufficient raw materials or insufficient production capacity, production request or allocation will be automatically replaced with the Sales volume x Individual potential demand / Aggregate potential demand for the respective market.

• Finished goods inventory can be sold in the respective market only.

● New equipment investment is expected to depreciate over the next 20 rounds (*i.e.*, 5 years).

If the production capacity cannot meet the total production request from each market, rationing of the supply of finished goods is needed and proportional to each of the market's requests with the following equation for actual production allocation.

Actual production allocation = Actual production volume x (Each market's production request) / (Total production request).

9. SUPPLY CHAIN

The Supply Chain (MBS > Analysis > Supply Chain) provides you with information such as Supply chain management cost, SCM cost as % of sales, SCM cost per unit sold, Profit margin as % of unit selling price, *etc.* (Fig. 7).

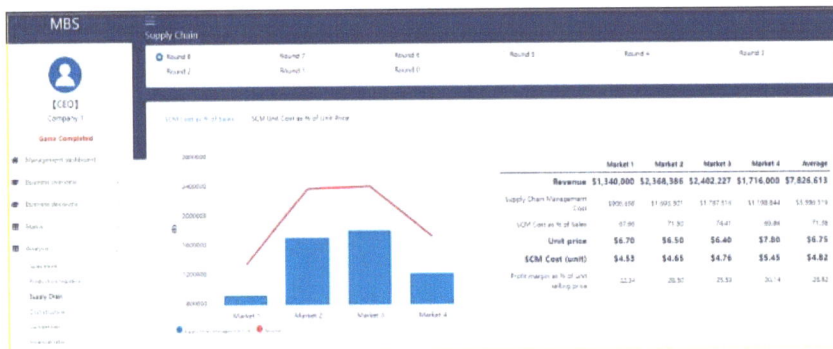

Fig. (7). Supply chain.

Supply chain management cost refers to the total cost of the flow of goods and services in a supply chain. SCM cost includes the movement and storage of raw materials of work-in-process inventory, labor, warehousing, transportation, sourcing, manufacturing expense, and finished goods as well as end-to-end order fulfillment from point of origin to point of consumption.

Total SCM cost as % of sales refers to the ratio of SCM cost to the total sales revenue = SCM cost / Total sales revenue.

SCM cost (unit) refers to the ratio of SCM cost to the sales quantity = SCM cost / Number of units sold.

SCM unit cost as % of unit selling price refers to the ratio of SCM unit cost to the unit price = SCM cost per unit / Unit selling price

Profit margin as % of unit selling price refers to the ratio of profit margin (defined by the unit selling price – SCM cost per unit sold) to the unit selling price = (Unit selling price – SCM cost per unit) / Unit selling price.

Fill rate: Sales volume / Potential demand.

Inventory days of supply: 365 / Inventory turnover = 365 x COGS / Average Inventory.

10. COST STRUCTURE

Cost Structure (MBS > Analysis > Cost Structure) provides you with information such as Cost of goods sold (unit), Gross profit margin (%), Operating expenses (unit), Management and financial expenses (unit), Operating profit EBIT (%), Variable cost, and Fixed Cost. Cost structure will help determine the breakeven point (units or dollar value) for selling in a certain market (Fig. **8**).

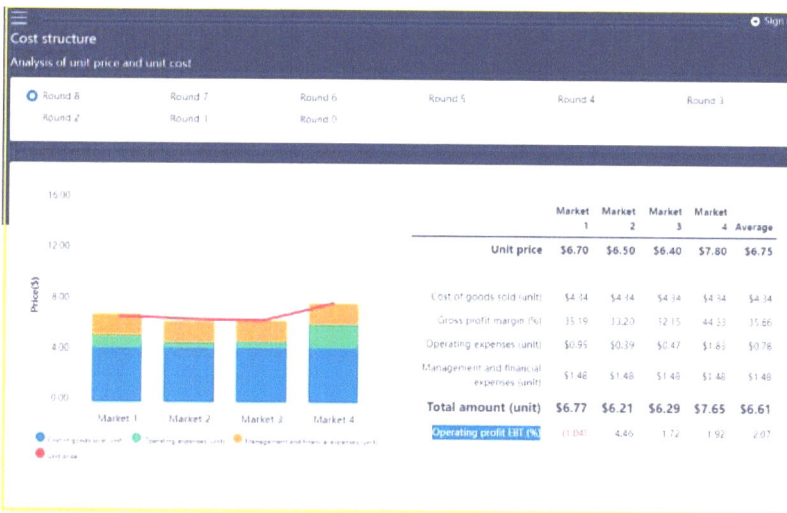

Fig. (8). Cost structure.

Cost of goods sold (unit) refers to the unit direct costs of producing the goods sold by a company. This amount includes the cost of the materials and labor directly used to create each unit of the finished good. It excludes indirect expenses, such as distribution costs and sales force costs.

Gross profit margin (%) refers to a measurement of profitability that shows the percentage of revenue that exceeds the COGS. The gross profit margin reflects how profitable it is for a company to generate revenue, considering the direct costs involved in producing their products and services.

Operating expense (unit) refers to other indirect costs associated with production and distribution activities, such as transportation, inventory, marketing expenses, *etc.*, divided by the number of units sold.

Management and financial expense (unit) refer to other expenses not directly related to the production and distribution activities. These costs include but are not limited to, expenses incurred for salary, management fees, and interest from the loan, *etc.*

Operating profit EBIT (%) refers to Earnings before interest and tax (EBIT) that measures a company's financial performance from its operations = (Revenue – All expenses excluding interest and taxes) / Revenue x 100%.

Variable cost is a direct cost that is traceable and changes in proportion to how much a company produces or sells. Variable costs increase or decrease depending on a company's production or sales volume.

Fixed cost refers to the indirect cost that does not change (or at least not significantly) regardless of the number of goods produced or sold.

11. CASE STUDY: SANITIZER

11.1. Overview

The business began as a Pharmacy focused on Hand Sanitizer for customers to prevent the spread of infections and decrease the risk of getting sick by applying your hands with at least 60% alcohol-based hand sanitizer. The retail shop of the pharmacy is located in the production and warehouse providing a financial income to the overall company and keeping pace with economic growth globally.

11.2. Ethanol (Raw Material)

Ethanol is used to produce hand sanitizer with a certain percentage of composition and the material conversion rate might be changed from the deterioration of the equipment quarterly to produce the hand sanitizer [2].

11.3. Hand Sanitizer (Finished Goods Product)

In the global health emergency caused by COVID-19, experts have mandated the use of hand sanitizers as a safety measure from COVID-19 to fight against the coronavirus [2].

11.4. Potential Customers

There could be a variety of reasons for exploring the customers purchasing the product from your firm. The main reasons are completely according to the customer's past purchasing experience. When you understand and recognize what your target customer desires for your quality, brand, and price, then you understand which in particular guides the whole customer journey. To keep loyal customers and attract new potential customers, firms are required to explore the key driving forces that encourage customers to buy hand sanitizer. In the post-pandemic period, firms are required to take into account various methods for customer experience because of the transformation in the marketplace.

12. STUDENT PLATFORM

ICETECH has designed and implemented Macro Business Simulation (MBS) Student Platform for students to form a group for knowledge exchange and play the MBS game. Fig. (**9**) shows the MBS student platform login page.

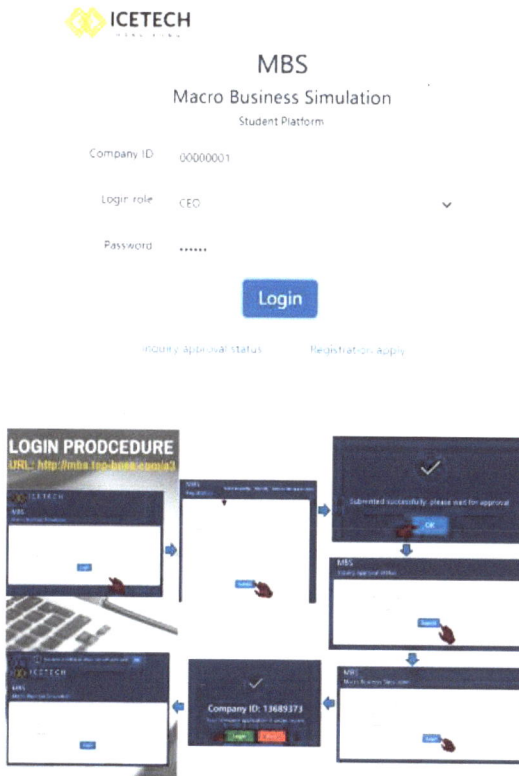

Fig. (9). Macro business simulation (MBS) student platform.

CONCLUSION

Macro business simulation games identify new innovative education tools because of the rise of innovative educational concepts and the emergence of online learning pedagogy. This chapter mainly recognizes the main elements of macro business simulation, and the core structures of macro business simulation, and points out the key expected students' learning outcomes. Furthermore, this chapter provides interdisciplinary knowledge about healthcare, education, and information technology.

REFERENCES

[1]   International association of business management simulation. Available from: https://www.intabms.org/ (accessed on 25 May 2023).

[2]   Lau YY, Dulebenets MA, Yip HT, Tang YM. Healthcare supply chain management under COVID-19 settings: The existing practices in Hong Kong and the United States. Healthcare 2022; 10(8): 1549. [http://dx.doi.org/10.3390/healthcare10081549] [PMID: 36011207]

SUBJECT INDEX

www.ingramcontent.com/pod-product-compliance
Lightning Source LLC
Chambersburg PA
CBHW080021240326
41598CB00075B/616